FOR

VISIONARIES, LEADERS & DREAMERS

PASSION, ENERGY, VALUES & VISION

Copyright ©2016 Shelley Wood

All rights reserved. No portion of this book may be used or reproduced in any manner whatsoever without written permission, except in the case of brief passages quoted in articles or reviews.
For information, address Lilac Grove Group LLC, 3739 Balboa Street 130, San Francisco, CA 94121

Managing Editor Ruth Tepper Brown
Developmental Editor Staci Backauskas
Designer Laura Jane Coats

ISBN 978-0-9984895-0-6

Publisher
Lilac Grove Group LLC

Shelley Wood is on a mission to create a new generation of joyful ChangeMakers who can tackle the myriad challenges facing our world today. Distilling twenty years of observation and study, she offers a head start to the next generation of leaders who want to make the world a better, more awake, and more self-aware place.

Experience has shown her that positive results can come from making tough decisions in ways that enhance connection, mitigate economic stress, and avert the breakdown of community. The ChangeMaker Guide celebrates great change leaders who have forged that more mindful path. It honors their legacies and reminds us that we each have the ability to create a better world—for ourselves, and for those around us. For more information visit shelley-wood.com.

FOR

VISIONARIES, LEADERS & DREAMERS

PASSION, ENERGY, VALUES & VISION

CONTENTS

Introduction
3

CHAPTER ONE

Where's the Passion?
Take time to explore what you care about
7

CHAPTER TWO

Finding the Energy
Expand and increase what energizes you
27

CHAPTER THREE

What's Really Important?
Discover your true values
59

CHAPTER FOUR

Paint Your Future
What does the future look like?
101

Quotes
133

Resources
141

I know
no one reads
the introduction.
I don't either...
usually.
But read this one.
Seriously.

Introduction

"The best way to learn is to teach."
EXPLORATORIUM FOUNDER DR. FRANK OPPENHEIMER

I was fortunate to work at the renowned San Francisco Exploratorium for eight years. There, hundreds of hands-on science exhibits offer the excitement of learning about the world through personal experience and unexpected discovery.

Although founder Frank Oppenheimer had been gone for some time before I joined the museum's staff, his spirit still permeated the place, and stories of how he navigated his world were legendary.

Frank liked to tell people that he lived on "the edge of chaos," a place between order and disorder—an environment that supported his need to create, explore, and play.

In this moment, many people live on the edge of chaos. The difference is we haven't learned how to use it like Frank did. We haven't yet grasped what Frank knew: that passion, purpose, and an open mind can turn the "edge of chaos" into a magical place where it's safe for us to explore and create something wonderful.

Nowhere is this truer today than in the world of business. The beliefs we've held about success, and what is necessary to obtain it, are crumbling. Some refer to the period we're currently in as the Information Age. In my vision, I see a new age on the horizon, something I call the Restoration of Community.

In many places, the sense of community that allows people to bring their whole selves to their work is missing. Fear of judgment and the possibility of negative consequences can keep people from reaching their true potential and sharing their unique creative gifts.

Only we have the power to restore community, but it will require a new generation of leaders. All it takes is one strong person being more open and inclusive to begin a transformation that will provide the roots for future change. Over time, changemakers who work to see the entire picture—including both the long-term and indirect consequences of their choices—will create better outcomes for us all.

Changemakers of the future need to understand that the connections created by technology are illusions. They need to realize that platforms like Facebook, Twitter, and Tumblr create isolation and narcissism more than community. In the end, we're still participating from a "safe" place behind our computers, tablets, and phones, rather than standing beside our neighbors and coworkers.

We need changemakers who are willing to see the entire picture, not merely the isolated sliver of the bottom line. True leaders have a vision extending beyond their own circle. True leaders consider our interdependency in making decisions, evaluating what's best for the whole.

We each have the ability to design better worlds for ourselves and for others, but it requires both commitment and strength to face off against a culture that continually reminds us of the price we may pay for going against the grain.

If you're up to that task, if you have a passion that drives you to change this world for the better, even if you have no idea how that will happen, this book is for you. It will offer you new ideas, connect you to valuable resources, and ask you to think about the trajectory of your life in ways you may never have considered before.

There are two things that may be helpful to you in understanding the way the book is organized:

■ Quotes meant to offer insight or inspiration are included in each chapter, but their citations are given at the back of the book. This arrangement allows you to consider each thought based on its own merits, rather than evaluating its validity according to its source.

■ Throughout the book you will find images of dragonflies and tortoises. The dragonflies signify the importance of being honest with yourself. The tortoises are reminders to slow down and reflect.

I hope you will be inspired by the ideas you find on these pages. I hope they will help you imagine new ways to envision your own journey and create a strong, supportive community. I hope this book will motivate you to dream big and begin moving along your true path, generating energy and empowering you to have the impact you were born to have.

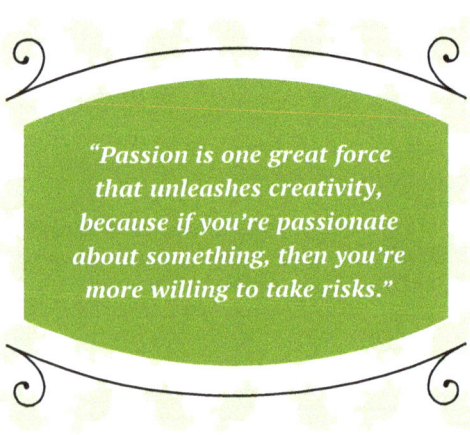

"Passion is one great force that unleashes creativity, because if you're passionate about something, then you're more willing to take risks."

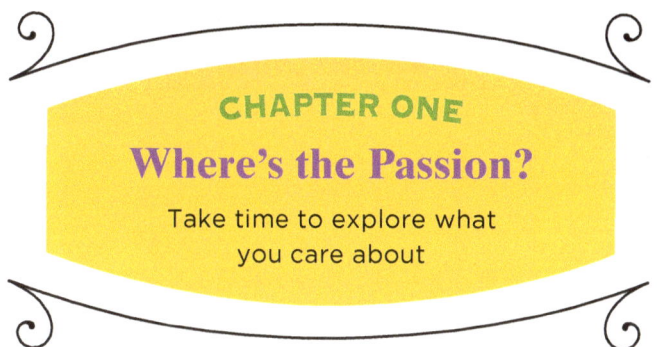

CHAPTER ONE
Where's the Passion?
Take time to explore what you care about

WHAT PASSION LOOKS LIKE

fter seven months of planning, I stood at the top of the grand staircase at the Carolands Chateau, just south of San Francisco, observing white-gloved waiters who were passing canapés beneath crystal chandeliers. A string quartet played lovely melodies while the wealthy guests mingled and drank champagne. Everything was in place for this important fundraiser. Almost.

My eyes scanned the crowd for the guest of honor. Just a few moments earlier, I had confessed to a colleague that I was afraid she wouldn't arrive on time—or that she might be too tired to inspire 200 philanthropists after traveling extensively for the past two days.

I was so relieved when I saw her enter the foyer. Like a whirlwind, she bounded up the stairs, two at a time, with the energy and excitement of a child. Suddenly, in front of me stood a fearless changemaker: marine biologist and savior of the oceans, Dr. Sylvia Earle.

In that moment, I knew there was nothing to worry about. Dr. Earle was 79 years old, but you wouldn't have known that to look at her. She was radiant, and it was obvious that she was excited to be there. I passed her a glass of

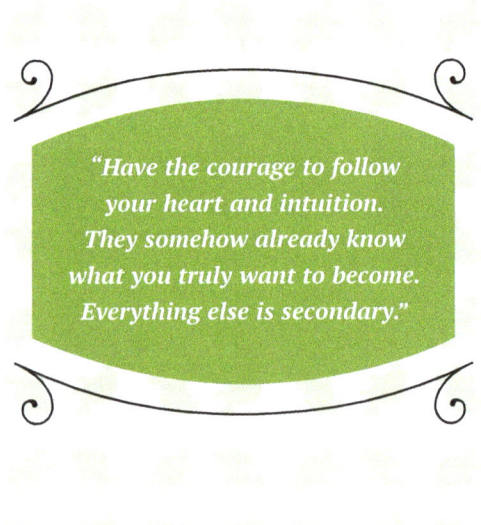

"Have the courage to follow your heart and intuition. They somehow already know what you truly want to become. Everything else is secondary."

chardonnay and asked, "Where on earth do you get all your energy?" She looked at me and said, "Imagine a baby." I looked puzzled, not sure where she was going with this. "Imagine the baby is falling from the sky. Now, imagine that you can catch that baby." Her eyes locked with mine. "Would you put your arms down even for a moment? Would you take a moment to rest?" She took a sip from the glass. "The ocean is my baby."

The passion Sylvia Earle has for protecting the ocean is motivated by her love for it. She travels more than 300 days a year, flying around the world to share the plight of the oceans and enrolling people in her cause. She works tirelessly to create a global network of marine protected areas called Hope Spots. She is not put off by the scale of the problem, nor does she limit herself to a specific goal. She does all she can every day to protect "her baby."

Sylvia Earle is one of the passionate ones. The ones who make a difference. The ones who have enormous energy, create great change, and convince others to jump on board. They are fearless. Resilient. And they are responsible for transformational change. When they are told there is no way forward, passionate people forge their own paths. They dedicate their lives to bringing something into creation. They see a need being ignored and work to improve the situation. Passionate people leave the planet and their communities in a better state than it would have been without them.

I had worried needlessly. Dr. Earle's speech was inspiring. After thunderous applause, she closed with, "I wish you would use all means at your disposal—films! expeditions! the web! more!—to ignite public support for a global network of marine protected areas, Hope Spots large enough to save and restore the ocean, the blue heart of the planet."

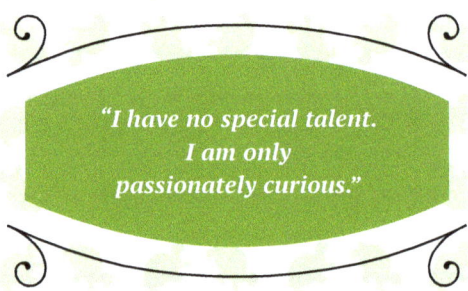

*"I have no special talent.
I am only
passionately curious."*

FINDING YOUR PASSION

fter graduating in 1900 as a teacher in mathematics and physics, Albert Einstein tried in vain to find a job as a professor in a university. If he had succeeded, he would never have ended up working as a technical assistant at the patent office in Bern, Switzerland. The work was relatively simple for him, and afforded him time to ponder his theories. This incubation time was much appreciated by Einstein, and he referred to the patent office as "a worldly cloister where I hatched my most beautiful ideas."

Like Einstein, you may not find your passion the way you think you will. It could be inspired by an innocent experience, or perhaps be something that has been in front of you for a long time. It might not come on the timetable you've established in your mind, and it rarely looks anything like what you might have imagined. All you can do, really, is take the next step toward it.

If you've been searching for a while and are worried that you don't know what your passion is yet, relax! If you feel you've lost your passion, relax! Maybe your perfect job hasn't been invented yet—or perhaps what you're doing right now is preparing you for bigger things to come.

The good news is that passions can change, so maybe it's time to explore new interests. It's okay if you don't know your purpose in life at this moment. What is important is to incorporate doing things you love into your life, even if it's only for a few minutes a day. Not all of us get the "lightning strike" that makes everything clear. Sometimes we ease into it.

You don't have to save the oceans to make an impact on this world. Great teachers, caregivers, volunteers, mentors, and leaders impact the lives of others for the better every day. Stay curious and enjoy the things that stimulate your

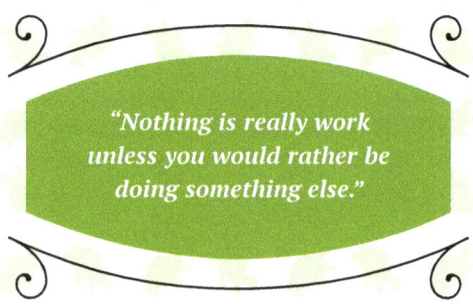

"Nothing is really work unless you would rather be doing something else."

mind, your heart, and your soul, and trust that the path will appear.

PASSION IN THE WORKPLACE

hen you love what you do, when you feel connected to your work and the people you work with, you can work hard and still have plenty of energy to do the things you love, and take care of the things you care about. Your efforts will lead to strong relationships and supportive cycles of connectedness.

Passionate people radiate life. They attract support and encourage and help others to be involved. Fundraisers know that people give to people, not organizations. Each interaction with a potential donor is one in which the likelihood of giving goes up or down depending on how someone associated with the organization makes them feel, whether it's an employee, a recipient of the organization's work, or an advocate.

People who have passion care about outcomes. When the going gets tough they don't give up. Instead, they find new ways to move forward. Passionate employees share their knowledge with everyone who will listen; their positivity and energy is contagious.

Experts who love learning also realize that great insights can come from novices. Novices may notice things that experts have become blind to. In fact, experts who have lost the ability to take on new ideas and learn new ways can be huge liabilities to innovation within organizations. People who are closed to learning lessons from other professions and communities may not be able to see the connections needed to make great leaps.

Passionate leaders often have transformational leadership styles, and transformational leaders create change for the

TIME TO SLOW DOWN AND REFLECT

QUESTIONS TO PONDER

What do you do that you admire ?

What are you good at ?

What would you like to be admired for ?

What are your strengths ?

What sections do you visit in bookstores ?

What are you like when you are at your best ?

What did you love to do at age seven ?

What do you enjoy when you have free time ?

What would you like to be good at ?

better. They work closely with their employees and make changes to create goals that are in line with the values of employees. They implement change by creating visions that are inclusive of group goals.

Transformational leaders often show emotion, and they encourage emotions from others. As a result, transformational leadership can increase employee satisfaction as they often see the organizational goals as their own. This meaningfulness will then increase employee passion. Even without direct reports or titles, transformational leaders can make changes that benefit themselves, their organizations, and their community.

Leaders who tap into their passion have increased energy, and this is essential to create transformational change. Passionate people help create a vision for others by communicating and sharing their knowledge and ideas. Painting this clear picture helps others effectively pursue goals toward this vision.

The word "collaborate" comes from the Latin *collaborare*, which means "to work together." True collaboration means setting aside your ego and working to achieve great outcomes. This is what passionate people do. They are part of a team that takes ownership of the outcome, collaborating for the greater good. Collaborative teams have spirit. They are resilient and agile.

Herman Maynard and Susan Mehrten's 1993 book *The Fourth Wave: Business in the 21st Century* (see Resources for complete citations) takes an in-depth look at the evolution of business, dividing the process into four "waves."

- The First Wave centers on agriculture. In it, people produce and exchange goods and services for mutual benefit.

- The Second Wave focuses on industrialization: Business

> *"Everything on Earth has a purpose, every disease an herb to cure it, and every person a mission. This is the Indian theory of existence."*

values are about profit, control, and survival; consumption is a key driver, and wealth is a measure of tangible assets with little regard for the environment.

■ The Third Wave focuses on the Information Age and the rise of technology, when people begin to take ethical, cultural, social, political, and economical environments into account.

■ Finally, in the Fourth Wave, business values emphasize stewardship for the whole, serving and creating value for everyone.

Visions and values of Fourth Wave business environments are aspirational for maintaining passion in the workplace, and important to emphasize here. In Fourth Wave business environments, managers are no longer needed; instead, leadership evolves with the needs of each project. Strongly shared values, principles, and vision drive decision-making. The use of technology is evaluated in context, and the environmental emphasis is on the preservation of all living systems. Social accounting—a mostly intangible outcome reflecting in quality of life—becomes the convention. But most importantly, the stakeholders include everyone and everything, all the people, creatures, and systems that interact across the planet.

American architect and influential thought leader William McDonough, who has built his firm to align with Fourth Wave principles, writes, "Our goal is a safe, healthy, and just world, with clean air, water, soil and power, economically, ecologically and elegantly enjoyed."

This is a vision that inspires passion in people. When they know they're doing something good, and their strengths are being harnessed to contribute to something worthwhile, they no longer need to be managed or told what to do. They will do what needs to be done.

> "We typically think of the leader as being the person at the top. But if you define a leader as an executive, then you absolutely deny everyone else in an organization the opportunity to be a leader."

WHAT A PASSIONATE TEAM LOOKS LIKE

From 2005 through 2013, I worked in Marketing and Institutional Advancement at the Exploratorium, a bustling, world-renowned, hands-on science center in San Francisco. It was often my job to help organize and manage public events, including Pi Day, an annual celebration that takes place on March 14 (corresponding to the mathematic term pi, which represents a number beginning with 3.14, and is, coincidentally, Einstein's birthday).

As a new employee, I was still learning how the museum worked when it became time to plan for the year's Pi Day activities. When I arrived at the kickoff meeting, I expected discussions to meander in typical fashion—lots of people sharing ideas and waiting for someone to take the lead and create a plan of action. It didn't take long for me to figure out that this team was different.

The leaders of the departments in attendance were passionate about Pi Day, first organized by the Exploratorium's fun-loving physicist, Larry Shaw. They came with ideas to make it the best Pi Day ever, and offered their expertise and time, not only to execute their own ideas, but to help other people's ideas come to fruition. People added to each other's thoughts and everyone collaborated. No one was in charge. No one needed to be. It was electric. We all knew how important Pi Day was to the Exploratorium's story and culture, and everyone took ownership of the outcome. We committed to creating a successful event and knew that if any problems came up, the team would be able to adapt and adjust.

This was so different from anything I'd experienced before. In the past, I'd only participated in Second Wave "collaborations," where the role of management was to serve

> *"Find out what you love.
> Do it because you love it.
> Stick with it. Start now."*

higher levels of management, and it was the responsibility of the event planner to assign staff to their respective roles. By contrast, Pi Day had soul. All the people involved in making it happen felt that and collaborated. The event was the only priority.

DESTROYING PASSION

Typically in Second Wave organizations, the roles are clarified, the expectations set, and the procedures put in place to give constructive feedback. Systems, not people, measure productivity and determine success. Those who carry out tasks well, reach certain goals, or behave in particular ways are externally rewarded with recognition, praise, or money. The role of a manager is to put these systems of accountability in place and execute them. If, in the process, issues arise and the system is blamed, then the focus becomes the system, not the people who are a part of it.

Accountability is important, but it is more beneficial to the organization and to the community as a whole when employees take some ownership for their work and the impact it has.

Passion is destroyed when accountability is more important than a sense of ownership around the outcome. When organizations grow (profits expand while stuck in the Second Wave mentality), rather than evolve, the focus is on establishing systems that organize and track people and their work. The belief is that this helps avoid redundancy and increase efficiency. But the more rigid and controlling these systems are, the less likely employees will have a sense of ownership, which means zero passion. It's possible to create an environment where people feel connected to each other and what they do. True leaders have the power to create environments of love, kindness, and collaboration.

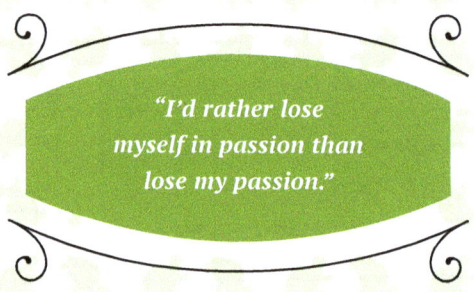

"I'd rather lose myself in passion than lose my passion."

THE PASSION SPECTRUM

 assion takes many forms. To be an effective leader it's important to know the range of what passion looks like and be able to recognize it.

■ Harmonious Passion: People who demonstrate harmonious passion have a love for something and it becomes a part of who they are. They spend significant time and energy on their passion, but still have time to do other things they enjoy. They are balanced and have healthy family and social lives.

People who have harmonious passion share their knowledge with those who seek it, and are open to new ways of looking at information. They're not afraid to try different approaches or methods. They are great assets in the workplace due to their abundance of energy. Their love for what they do is contagious. Their lives, and those of others are enhanced by the work they do.

■ Obsessive Passion: People who demonstrate obsessive passion work hard, but they are sometimes so compulsively focused on their work that they become unaware of what is going on around them. They will often take on extensive workloads and allow other parts of their lives to suffer.

Those with this type of passion can be less open-minded. They also tend to be inflexible and many have tunnel vision. They are skeptical about other viewpoints and new ways of doing things.

People who have obsessive passion can be dangerous in organizations because they may perceive themselves as the hardest workers. Yet their work is often ineffective, and their attitudes can have a negative impact on others.

■ Brownout: The final hue on the passion spectrum is called brownout. This is even more dangerous to organizations

TIME TO SLOW DOWN AND REFLECT

DO YOU HAVE
HARMONIOUS PASSION?

Is your work enjoyable?
Do you have a sense of flow?
Are you energized after working?
Do you have energy for other things you care about?

DO YOU HAVE
OBSESSIVE PASSION?

Is what you are doing truly important?
Are you open to new ways?
Are you always exhausted?
Are you neglecting relationships?

DO YOU HAVE
BROWNOUT?

Have you lost passion for your work?
Are you closed to new ideas?
Is efficiency your top priority?
Do you block ideas?

than burnout. When you or one of your team members are in burnout, it's obvious. You see the signs of people being overcommitted or overworked. If you choose to pay attention to the signs, you can take steps to remedy it, from hiring more staff and encouraging breaks to introducing techniques like meditation and implementing morale boosters.

Brownout, on the other hand, is not as recognizable. It's hard to spot because those suffering from it turn up to work, say the right things, and still produce. They are reliable. They are often the go-to person at the organization. Their knowledge of infrastructure and politics enables them to find workarounds rather than addressing problems that need to be solved.

People with brownout passion are sometimes viewed as the superstars of an organization, which can be doubly dangerous. They don't bring their whole selves to work, and therefore are not engaged or able to bring out the best in others. They don't seek new opportunities. More importantly, their seniority and influence can prevent new initiatives from getting off the ground, which can be detrimental to the organization. This happens because they have lost touch with their passion and what drives them. Having given up on change, they carry out their roles without worrying about what is happening around them, blind to the broader impact their attitudes make. The price for their reliability is a lack of innovation.

> "I sincerely believe that energy grows from itself and the more energy you expend the more you create within yourself. I also believe energy is a habit which can be created quite easily. In other words, use your energy and more energy flows and then it is very hard to stop—as if one would ever want to!"

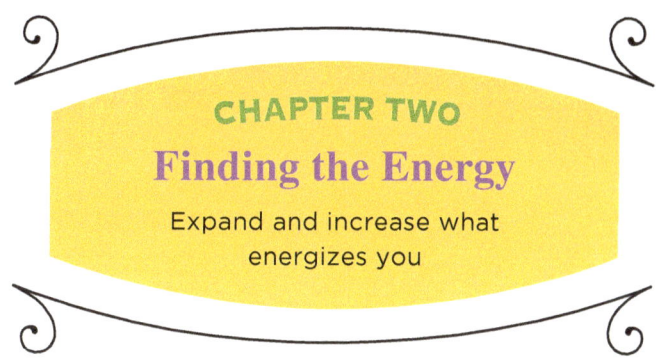

CHAPTER TWO
Finding the Energy
Expand and increase what energizes you

A HAIKU ON ENERGY

*If you're searching for
reasons to do something, you
don't want to do it*

Home from university on holiday, I was ready to go out for an evening of fun when I found my mother ironing socks. In Walsall, the town where I grew up in England's industrial West Midlands, people ironed everything—towels, underwear, sheets. Even socks. "Come with me to the pub," I offered. "I'm ready for a drop of grog."

She turned to me, still committed to removing the wrinkles from socks, and said, "I wish I had time to gallivant off like you. I don't have time." I could feel her bad mood. "But Mom," I said, "you're ironing socks." She returned to her ironing and I headed out to meet my friends.

My mother didn't necessarily like ironing socks, yet she did it. Why? Because we all do things we don't want to do simply because we've absorbed the energy around what it means to do them. This forms a perception that can easily solidify into a belief of what is right, what it means if we don't do something, and the fear of the consequences we'll experience for "rebelling."

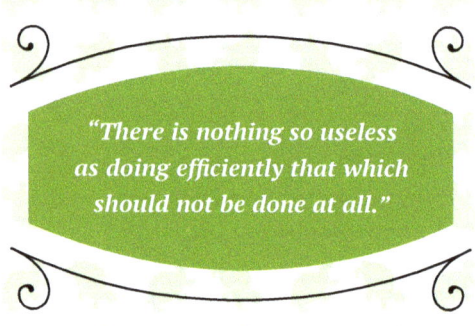

"There is nothing so useless as doing efficiently that which should not be done at all."

Mom's sense of self, her very identity, came from being a good mother. This meant she had to do the things good mothers do. My grandmother ironed socks. My aunts ironed socks. To this day, my sister irons socks, as I'm sure many of my cousins do. Ironing socks was something good mothers did.

She learned this from her mother, who learned it from hers. Yes, it became a belief—even if it was an unconscious one—but it started with the energy. My mom probably learned that ironing socks was one of the things good mothers did without my grandmother ever saying a word.

My mom didn't think about ironing socks. It was just something that had to be done. She never stopped to question it. She just did it. She didn't ask what would happen if it didn't get done or what she could do with that time instead. She didn't ask if someone else could do it.

That evening, home from school and barely an adult, I just wanted my mom to come out with me for a whiskey and lemonade. I didn't understand that even she didn't understand why she was so driven to iron everything. In my ignorant youth, I thought she was being ridiculous. Who irons socks?

The truth is, socks don't need to be ironed. If it brings you joy, then go for it. But people do things every day just because it's what they think they should do without ever considering why they're doing it. Maybe it fits with the image they want to portray. Or perhaps it's the fear of what will happen if they don't do it that drives them. Regardless of why, it all starts with energy.

The bottom line is, don't spend time doing things that drain your energy or put you in a bad mood. And don't spend time doing things that don't need to be done. As management consultant Peter Drucker says, "There is nothing so

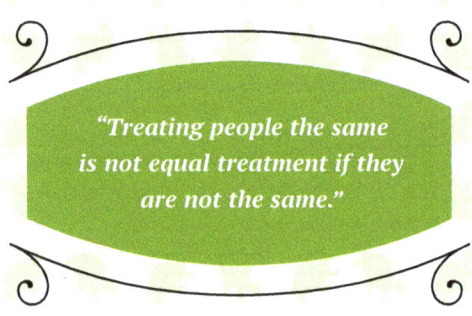

"Treating people the same is not equal treatment if they are not the same."

useless as doing efficiently that which should not be done at all." By contrast, spending just a small amount of time doing what you love can really energize you.

WHAT IS ENERGY?

 hat is energy? If you ask scientists, they may tell you that energy is "*mc* squared." But for our purposes, it's the nonverbal output of an interaction.

For example, imagine you're at a party and the hostess tells you she wants to introduce you to one of her friends. She raves about the person on your way to the introduction. When her friend smiles at you, he exudes delight at meeting you. The energy is electric, and you leave the party feeling happy. Now imagine you're at the same party, and you get in line behind someone at the buffet who looks down his nose at the selections available. He bumps into the person in front of him and doesn't acknowledge it. Then he sniffs everything before he puts it on his plate. How do you feel about him? Chances are, you're not going to sit at his table. He hasn't said a word, but you've received the energy he's giving off, and it's not something you want to be around.

We all absorb the energy of others and are impacted by the energy of those around us. It may sound existential, but it's something we all experience. Some of us are better than others in deflecting the negative energy around us, but we can all be impacted by an environment of negative energy. That's why it's important to surround yourself with supportive, positive energy.

The ability to identify and manage your own energy, and the energy of the teams you work with, is critical to being a successful leader. Energy is the unspoken factor that other people feel, even if they can't articulate what they're

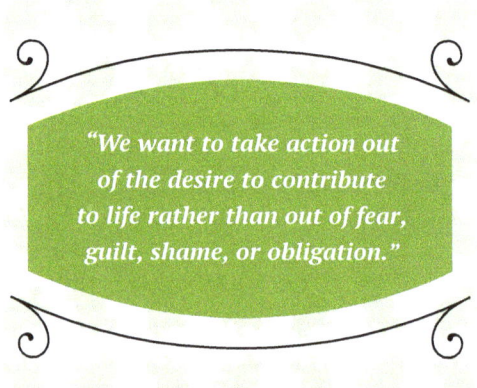

"We want to take action out of the desire to contribute to life rather than out of fear, guilt, shame, or obligation."

feeling. The energy of resentment is just as potent as the energy of enthusiasm.

Psychologist Marshall Rosenberg, author of the book *Nonviolent Communication: A Language of Life*, tells a wonderful story of a time when he was coaching parents on how to communicate better with their children. He was discussing words he didn't feel were valuable when dealing with children: words like "you must" and "you should."

A mother stood up and said, "That's ridiculous. Sometimes, you must do what you don't want to."

"Please give me an example," Marshall asked.

"I don't want to cook dinner, but I do it every night," she said.

In this example, the activity of cooking dinner aligned with this woman's self-concept as a mother, as well as what it meant to her to be a good wife and parent. As a result of Marshall's coaching, she went home and told her family she was not going to cook dinner anymore.

Two weeks later, her eldest sons came to another of Marshall's workshops and he asked them, "How did you feel when your mother said she wasn't cooking dinner anymore?"

"I felt great," responded the eldest child. "This means she won't be complaining about cooking all through dinner."

When people do things they don't want to do, someone always the pays the price... eventually. If you are instead driven by what interests you—a sense of curiosity and a need to learn, teach, or create—you may reach a place where your desires intersect with your ability to control your own life. You are doing something because you want to, not because you have to, and it brings you joy and a sense of accomplishment. This is the road to true happiness.

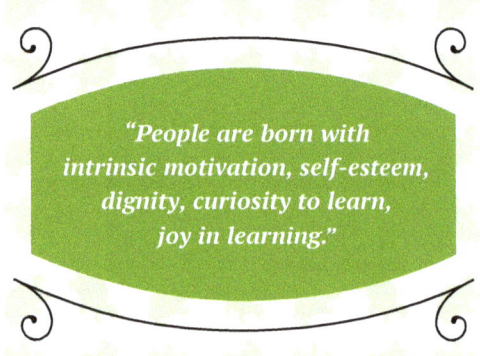

"People are born with intrinsic motivation, self-esteem, dignity, curiosity to learn, joy in learning."

So stop ironing socks, cooking dinner, or the equivalent of whatever sucks up your energy, and find a positive outlet for your efforts.

THE EFFECT OF FAIRNESS ON ENERGY

veryone has an inbuilt sense of right and wrong. Psychologist Paul Bloom's research at the Yale Infant Cognition Center found that this moral compass is innate, something we're born with. We don't need to learn a sense of justice or how to make judgements about people and situations. We do it before we can even speak.

This human quality is what leads to our definition of fairness, which is sometimes agreed upon by others and sometimes not. In a team or business situation, however, structure comes with rules, and when those rules—whether verbalized or not—are broken without consequence, we perceive that an "unfairness" has occurred.

Ethics professor Jerald Greenberg has identified the types of results that can occur when team members feel they're being treated unfairly. These include reduction in performance, emotional exhaustion, and decreased levels of trust among team members and managers. Even if these issues begin with just one person, this divisive energy can eventually spiral out and affect other team members.

The issue with "fairness" is that it can mean different things to different people. In traditional organizations, rules are implemented that often serve no other purpose than to create structure. They don't take into account the needs and desires of individual team members. Sometimes, rules are practical. Only one person can get the promotion. Only one person can be hired for the job. There is only enough money to send two employees to a conference.

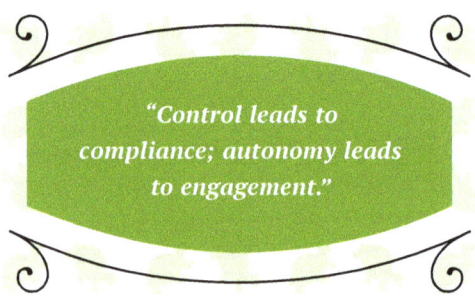

"Control leads to compliance; autonomy leads to engagement."

There are plenty of other instances, however, where treating everyone with the same rules doesn't make any sense. For example, the rule in your organization may be that no one who's worked for the company less than a year may attend a conference. But does it make more sense to send the friendly, outgoing team member—the consummate networker—who's only been there six months, or the introverted employee who's been with the organization for six years?

Well-intentioned managers follow the rules without asking or caring if those rules make any sense. It may seem that rules put in place in the name of fairness will make everyone happy, but in fact they're just as likely to make everyone unhappy, since personal needs can never be met. You should be able to allow an employee to carry a cell phone if they're dealing with a seriously ill family member, even if "no cell phones on the public floor" is the rule. You should be able to allow an employee to shift a lunch break if childcare issues come up, even if lunch is always supposed to be at a set time.

These kinds of decisions, however, fly in the face of conventional business practice. Without some flexibility in dealing with individuals, one employee can be seen as being the same as another — ultimately interchangeable, and so easily replaceable. When team members feel their needs are being met, and that they have some control over what they do, it doesn't really matter if someone else receives something they don't. That only becomes a focus when employees are feeling undervalued and unconsidered.

Yes, it's important to be fair in some arenas. Treating all team members with dignity and courtesy, with respect and lack of prejudice, is critical. Providing clear and consistent explanations of the processes within an organization is essential. Being truthful about special rules and consideration

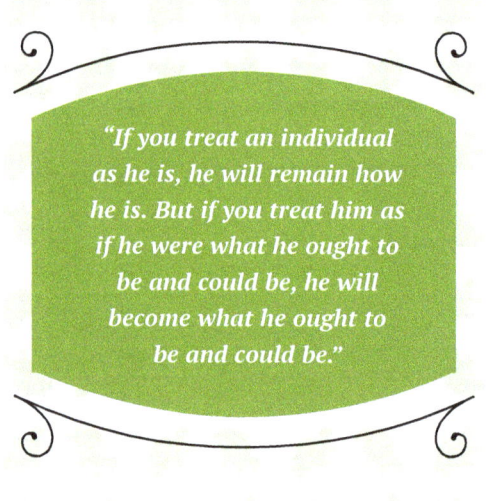

"If you treat an individual as he is, he will remain how he is. But if you treat him as if he were what he ought to be and could be, he will become what he ought to be and could be."

goes a long way in building trust because, as humans, we require a degree of fairness in how we are treated as compared to our coworkers. We use it as a proxy for trust.

People who are effective leaders spend more time building trust, and making others feel special for their unique abilities, than focusing on restrictive procedural policies. When you provide for a team member's needs — even if it doesn't make sense to offer those provisions to everyone else — that person will be less concerned about "fairness" when allowances need to be made for others. Teams come together when members understand that it's better in the long run when individuals have opportunities suited to them, rather than insisting everyone receive fewer privileges because of a "rule." A team that is solid is effective and productive, and that creates an energy that is felt by everyone.

THE ENERGY OF MOTIVATION

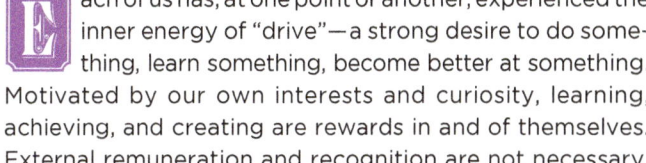ach of us has, at one point or another, experienced the inner energy of "drive"— a strong desire to do something, learn something, become better at something. Motivated by our own interests and curiosity, learning, achieving, and creating are rewards in and of themselves. External remuneration and recognition are not necessary. Setbacks do not stop the desire to move forward.

This energy, which comes from within, is persistent and committed. A toddler doesn't give up attempting to walk after the first, fifth, or even the hundredth time, even if she falls. She'll try to run just to experiment. She won't be held back by anxiety or fear. I have seen how those with this intrinsic motivation experience increased physical and psychological wellbeing.

In their study of human behavior, E. L. Deci and R. M. Ryan developed the Self-Determination Theory (SDT) in 1985.

TIME TO SLOW DOWN AND REFLECT

IDENTIFY YOUR MOTIVATION LEVEL

WHICH TYPE BEST DESCRIBES YOU ?

AMOTIVATION

I have no motivation
I have no energy
I have no self-determination

EXTRINSIC MOTIVATION

I do things out of a sense of guilt
I do things out of a sense of duty
I do things as a means to an end
I do things that align with my identity

INTRINSIC MOTIVATION

I do things because I want to
I do things that feel right to me
I do things just for enjoyment
I do things out of curiosity

They argued that a person's most important psychological need was self-determination, which is the ability to make decisions for yourself without influence from the outside. The more self-determination you have, the more intrinsically motivated you are. Their theory describes a continuum ranging from amotivation to extrinsic motivation and, finally, to intrinsic motivation, all of which are valuable for leaders to understand.

- Amotivation: Amotivation is no motivation at all. With no energy or willingness to do anything, there is no self-determination.

- Extrinsic Motivation: Extrinsic motivation sometimes has a very low level of self-determination. This is where you do something specifically to get something in return. Self-determination is also low when you are doing something out of guilt or duty, even though you don't want to do the task (like cooking dinner or ironing socks).

Extrinsic motivation, however, can also include elements of self-determination in situations where you do something you don't want to do because it's a step toward something bigger. For example, you may hate math, but you take a math class because you want to get into medical school. You see the activity as a means to an end.

Extrinsic motivation has high self-determination when you do something you don't want to do because it aligns with your values and true concept of yourself. Be aware, though, that this can be dangerous and lead to feelings of negativity or resentment when things don't go as planned. If you find yourself in this position, you might ask yourself if there's another way to get what you want.

- Intrinsic motivation: Intrinsic motivation is when you are driven to do something because you truly want to. You're curious, or you believe it's the right thing to do; you aren't seeking outside validation or reward.

TIME TO SLOW DOWN AND REFLECT

YOUR AUTONOMY PROFILE

DO YOU SUPPORT AUTONOMY?

I give people choices
I offer positive, non-controlling feedback
I do not micromanage
I provide flexibility where possible

DO YOU SUPPORT GROWTH?

I'm open to new ways
I help others find new ways
I set challenging goals
I express confidence in others

DO YOU ENCOURAGE RELATEDNESS?

I am encouraging and supportive
I listen attentively to personal disclosures
I display genuine affection to others
I show my true self to people

Intrinsic motivation is often thought only to apply to leisure activities you enjoy, like painting, playing golf, or gardening. The interesting thing about activities like these is that, at times, it can appear as though the motivation is strictly intrinsic, when the truth is that the external reward— a completed painting, a great golf handicap, or growing prizewinning roses—also factors in. Intrinsic motivation is present when the only reward for doing something is the act, and personal enjoyment, of doing it.

As a leader, when you identify that someone on your team is intrinsically motivated, it's important to let that be enough. Studies have shown that when external rewards are offered for activities that are already internally rewarding, those additional rewards can make the activity less intrinsically rewarding through a phenomenon known as the "overjustification effect."

In his text *Psychology: A Concise Introduction*, Richard A. Griggs explains that the addition of extrinsic reinforcement may cause someone to perceive a task as overjustified, which can lead to "an attempt to understand their true motivation. This then mitigates, and sometimes eliminates, the sense of internal reward."

AUTONOMY AND INSTRINSIC MOTIVATION

Business professors Marylène Gagné and Devasheesh Bhave, in their book *Human Autonomy in Cross-Cultural Context*, wrote a chapter delineating the positive effects of autonomy in the workplace. Providing autonomy for employees can increase job satisfaction, resilience, and a willingness to try new things. It usually enhances workplace performance because individuals who feel they're part of a collective are more likely to take responsibility for organizational outcomes.

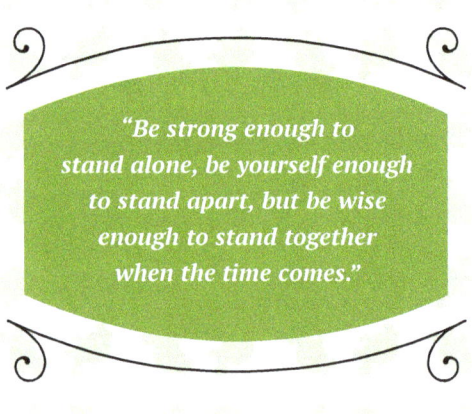

> *"Be strong enough to stand alone, be yourself enough to stand apart, but be wise enough to stand together when the time comes."*

Autonomy plays a large role in job satisfaction. If it doesn't exist, turnover and absenteeism are often higher. There can be lower levels of accountability and a general lack of team spirit. A lack of autonomy can also create a sense of employee helplessness.

Environments with low levels of autonomy are typically found in highly centralized, bureaucratic systems, and are also common in organizations where impossible goals are set and rewards, especially monetary rewards, are given without a connection to performance. These kinds of environments condition employees to expect the worst and become passive about taking initiative. In the worst cases, it can lead to anxiety and depression.

To inspire the most from your team, it's important to improve workplace autonomy. It seems simple enough, yet every day managers with good intentions reduce their employees' sense of autonomy rather than increasing it. Managers often take precautions, especially on a new project or with a new team, to eliminate the possibility of mistakes. They give detailed instructions for a task and then end up doing it themselves. Why do managers, who should know better, manage like this?

Travis Bradberry, author of *Emotional Intelligence 2.0*, tells us that it comes from our fight or flight response. Due to the high pressure that is common in today's workplaces, deadlines are likely to evoke some level of anxiety. Bradberry tells us, "A trigger event, such as a new deadline to meet, is 'felt' by the limbic system before we have any rational reaction to the circumstance. We fully experience the anxiety, exuberance, or irritation of a moment before the rational part of the brain has a chance to choose a response to the situation. So the manager reacts to her anxiety about trusting the abilities of her team members. She is likely unaware of this emotion, and doesn't recognize the impact of her actions on those around her."

TIPS FOR INCREASING AUTONOMY

INCREASED AUTONOMY IN THE WORKPLACE IS ACCOMPLISHED IN A NUMBER OF WAYS

Step back and don't micromanage

Involve the whole team in goal setting

Allow people to evaluate their own performances

Seek input and feedback from your employees

Communicate your intentions

Provide flexible working conditions

Explain the decision-making process

Offer options whenever possible

In this situation, Bradberry's advice is for the manager to make an effort to manage her own emotions. With a more nuanced understanding of the situation, she would not feel compelled to fight or take control to make sure all the work is done. Instead, she could be there to monitor the progress of the team and help where needed. Then, she could use team meetings, or other team-oriented situations, as opportunities to recalibrate so deadlines are met without stepping in and doing everything herself.

THE ENERGY OF EMOTION

Emotional intelligence, or EI, is a phrase that has garnered a lot of buzz over the last few years because the experts have finally realized that emotion—energy in motion—affects us all, whether we're on a team in a business setting or donating time as a volunteer. But what exactly is emotional intelligence, and how do you increase it?

EI helps quantify the unquantifiable concept of emotion. It can't be measured or put into a Petri dish, yet it plays a huge role in how we interact with others. Preston Ni, author of more than two dozen books on emotion and human behavior, defines EI as the "ability to understand, manage, and effectively express one's own feelings, as well as engage and navigate successfully with those of others."

According to Travis Bradberry (whose firm, Talent Smart, works with organizations like Coca Cola and the U.S. Army to increase their employees' EI), ninety percent of high performers in the workplace possess high EI, while eighty percent of low performers have low EI.

How do you increase your emotional intelligence quotient, or EQ? Preston Ni offers six essential areas in which you must increase your abilities in order to raise your EI:

TIPS
FOR INCREASING AUTONOMY

YOU CAN MAKE A DIFFERENCE IN CREATING SUPPORTIVE CONNECTIONS

Be friendly and considerate

Hold team-building sessions

Emphasize group values and goals

Remember personal details

Make after-work meet-ups optional

Personalize messages

Coach and mentor

Have multiple ways to participate

Socialize new employees

- Reduce negative emotions
- Manage stress
- Express difficult emotions
- Stay proactive around difficult people
- Bounce back after setbacks
- Express intimate emotions

The last one can be especially difficult because learning to communicate uncomfortable feelings is not something we're taught to do in modern society. Holding those feelings in and not communicating to others on your team or in management leads to a buildup of resentment. We all know that doesn't typically end well.

Ni suggests using the XYZ formula ("I feel X when you do Y in situation Z") as a way to frame difficult emotions when communicating them to others. He also recommends not starting sentences with "you," as they can make a listener defensive. This makes it more likely that the person to whom you're talking is thinking of ways to counter what you're saying rather than listening.

Honest and compassionate communication around emotions is essential to being a great leader. Take the time to explore your own EQ and invest the energy to raise it.

GROWTH, THE PERPETUAL ENERGY

Most humans have a need to feel competent, even masterful. Whether it's selling the most widgets or shaving thirty seconds off your running time, it's an important piece of a person's self-esteem.

Leaders are charged with the responsibility of motivating growth and learning in members of their team. What I've discovered is that there is really only one effective way of doing this, and I learned it at the tender age of 11 on holiday with my parents.

> *"The happiness of a man in this life does not consist in the absence but in the mastery of his passions."*

We were in Malta sitting round a hotel pool when an American family arrived and sat near us. One of their children was terrified of the water and could not swim. The parents were loud with praise: "You're so amazing putting on your arm bands! You did great touching the water!"

I come from a family of people watchers, so at first we found this amusing, and also, if I'm honest, a bit odd. But within a week, that little girl could not only swim, she also readily jumped into the deep end and swam across the full length of the pool. Underwater. When we learn a new skill or exceed our expectations around performance, we satisfy our need for competency and mastery.

There are three things that drive our desire to learn new skills and accomplish new tasks. The first two are internally competing motivations: the possibility of success, and the need to protect ourselves from loss or failure. Both push us to be better.

The third component critical to our growth is external motivation. Had that girl's parents chastised her for what she could not do, rather than encouraging her with praise for what she could do, as silly as it may have seemed to me as a girl, the results would not have been the same. In fact, she most likely would not have succeeded. She may even have ended up with lifelong issues around swimming.

There are several factors that determine whether or not we seek out new challenges. These can be strong enough to suppress the need for mastery and the competence that encourages growth. As a leader, it's vital to pay attention to those on your team to see where they fit in.

People who have had previous success with challenges will readily take them on again, but those who have failed—especially those who have experienced the kind of failure that resulted in ridicule or shame—will probably

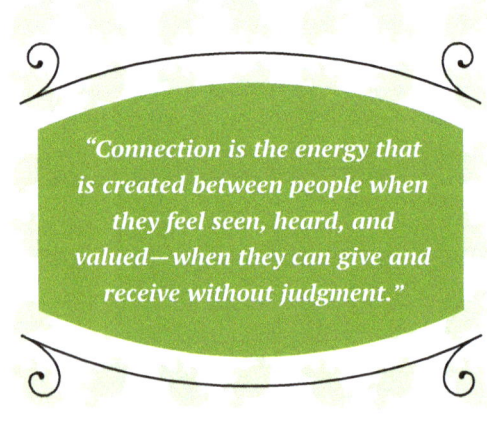

"Connection is the energy that is created between people when they feel seen, heard, and valued—when they can give and receive without judgment."

avoid future challenges. Independent people with high, but realistic, standards are more likely to be motivated to achieve, as will people who come from backgrounds that value achievement.

In addition to understanding the learning styles of your team members, there are a few ways you can increase their motivation to learn and grow. Make tasks specific and challenging. Ensure there is friendly competition. And, finally, offer constructive, positive feedback, expressing confidence in the person's ability to succeed.

A healthy environment is also essential for higher achievement motivations. An environment that fosters a sense of being valued, and that contributes to employee self-esteem, will see higher achievement motivation and greater effort.

Another critical factor is "flow." This is a self-created environment—one where competence and challenge meet. When a challenge exceeds someone's level of competence, that person can get frustrated and feel stressed. Conversely, if someone's level of competence exceeds the expectations of a challenge, that person is likely to become bored. When you can create a place for yourself where your competence supports the challenge, even if it's a little uncomfortable at times, you'll feel energized. Being in this state of flow means you're able to work for a really long time because you're invigorated by the challenge and your confidence in being able to overcome it.

THE ENERGY OF CONNECTION

There is a desire in all human beings to interact with others to some extent and to establish positive and genuine relationships. Quality and not quantity is important. In the workplace, it's vital to have opportunities for positive relationships to be cultivated with supervisors, peers, subordinates, clients, customers, vendors, and so on.

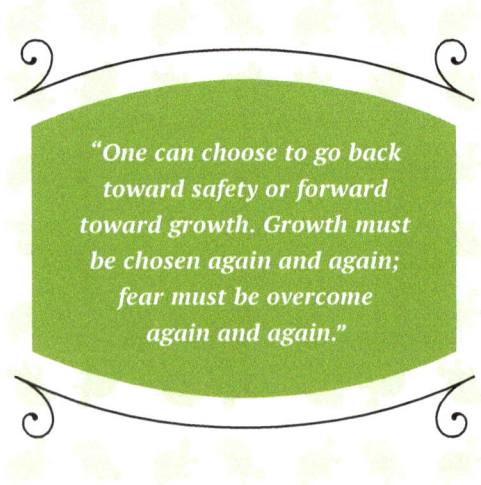

"One can choose to go back toward safety or forward toward growth. Growth must be chosen again and again; fear must be overcome again and again."

The more positive and genuine relationships that exist within an organization, the better the quality of the organizational citizenship will be. As a result, individual agendas become less of a priority.

Although it can't always be quantified, and is often more of a feeling, the energy of connection or relatedness can create positive social exchange, in addition to economic exchange. Social exchanges can create mutual trust and respectful relationships, whereas economic exchanges will create only quid-pro-quo relationships.

Psychologist Abraham Maslow's theory of a Hierarchy of Needs has been used as the basis for workplace research since the 1960s. His concept that "belonging" is the most important need after physiological and safety needs are met supports the idea that feeling connected and related is crucial in creating a healthy work environment. Today, it's becoming even harder to satisfy that need as virtual work and telecommuting become more common. The effects of not feeling connected can be devastating.

In 2008, psychologists D.L. Ferris, D.J. Brown, J.W. Berry, and H. Lian developed the Workplace Ostracism Scale. Although it focuses mostly on the effects of being purposely ignored or excluded by coworkers, it translates well to the disconnection experienced by so many workers today. The result of being ignored or excluded is a feeling of disconnection or not belonging. The consequences Ferris and his colleagues identified include poor mental health (especially anxiety), decreased physical health, low job satisfaction and commitment, and high counterproductive behavior and withdrawal.

On the flip side, studies on the benefits of feeling connected have been illuminating. A 1996 study, published in the U.S. National Library of Medicine, found that patients undergoing coronary bypass surgery had better recovery rates when their roommates had undergone the same surgery.

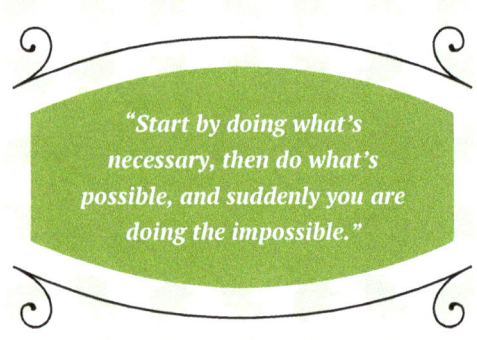

"Start by doing what's necessary, then do what's possible, and suddenly you are doing the impossible."

Sharing a room with someone who had not had the same surgery, or having no roommate at all, increased recovery time and decreased the quality of improvement.

Creating an environment where all members of a team feel connected and can relate to fellow workers benefits everyone. It increases intimacy and fulfills the need for warm and positive relationships with others. It helps to reduce feelings of rejection or anxiety because it nurtures inclusiveness. It stimulates a genuine interest in others and satisfies the human need for belonging, approval, acceptance, and security.

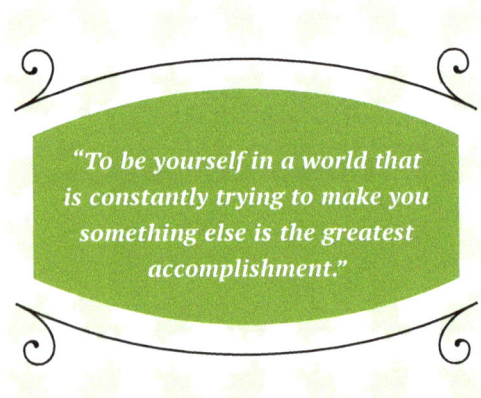

"To be yourself in a world that is constantly trying to make you something else is the greatest accomplishment."

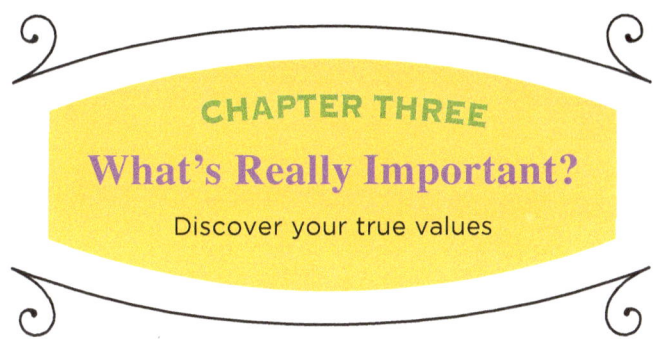

CHAPTER THREE
What's Really Important?
Discover your true values

DISCOVERING WHAT'S REALLY IMPORTANT

Throughout the course of history, the concept of self-knowledge, of knowing who you are, has been explored by our most revered thinkers, philosophers, and leaders. From Plato and Socrates to Maslow and Myers-Briggs, the variety of paths available to acquire that knowledge has been discussed and analyzed in a myriad of ways.

Each of us possesses three different threads that, when braided together, comprise the whole of who we are: personality, experience, and values. Knowing what your own unique set of characteristics is plays a vital role in your ability to become and remain a changemaker.

Values help you understand what you need, and what is important to you. Personality dictates how you demonstrate those values. Your experiences provide the path. Being aware of your values, your personality, and your experiences creates a kaleidoscope of opportunity for you to live a fulfilling life that has an impact not only on you, but on the world.

> "Authentic values are those by which a life can be lived, which can form a people that produces great deeds and thoughts."

PERSONALITY

I remember, as early as age six, how curious I was, always wanting to know why things were the way they were. I drove my mother crazy with questions, never being satisfied with the pat answers usually tolerated by a child. I wanted details! As soon as I had an acceptable answer, I was on to a new experience, afraid I might miss something if I stood still too long.

So many of my childhood memories are centered on the love of the unknown. I pressed elevator buttons just to see what would happen, and once took apart a Muppet sponge toy so I could see what was inside. I loved to mix things together—once it was talcum, salt, and flower petals—and did so with a large amount of optimism, convinced that I could make something wonderful. I always jumped right into a project to see what would happen.

When I got a bit older, I volunteered with a county community program to take care of the environment during summer vacation. I traveled by bus with other volunteers to places in the area that needed overgrowth cleared, steps repaired, and other conservation work done. Yes, it helped to make the community more beautiful, but if I'm being honest, it was all about exploring what I didn't know.

I see clearly now how the personality traits I use today to support individuals and organizations who want to do good have been with me for a long time. I'm certain that, if you thought about your own experiences, you too could make the connection between your passion and your personality, which is established very early in life.

For years, the Jesuits have followed the philosophy of St. Francis Xavier: Give me a child until he is seven, and I will give you the man. In essence, this says that your personality is formed by the time you enter second grade.

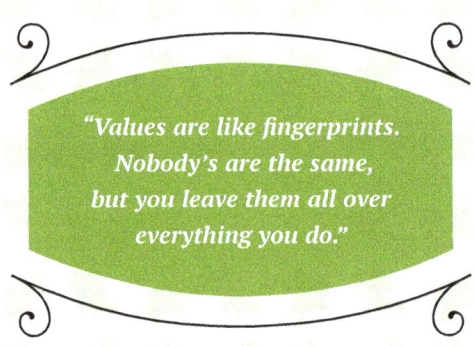

"Values are like fingerprints. Nobody's are the same, but you leave them all over everything you do."

There have been other studies done that empirically confirm this long-held belief. One, conducted by doctoral candidate Christopher Nave at the University of California, Riverside, determined that we remain recognizably the same person across our life span, and that the traits we exhibit as early as first grade are a good predictor of adult behavior.

Think about that for a minute. The first seven years of your life establishes who you become.

There are many ways to analyze, evaluate, and assess your personality traits and discover the positives and negatives of each. In fact, there are four well-known tools that focus on just that endeavor.

■ Myers-Briggs Type Indicator: Originally published in 1944, the Myers-Briggs Type Indicator is one of the best known personality assessment tools. Created by Katharine Cook Briggs and her daughter, Isabel Briggs Myers, it is deeply rooted in Jungian theory. Both a psychiatrist and a psychotherapist, Carl Jung theorized that humans experience the world through four channels: sensation, intuition, feeling, and thinking. He believed that only one of these channels was dominant for most of each person's lifetime. This tool asks you to select your preference from a series of choices, with the answers forming the building blocks for your personality type, offering a better understanding of your interests, needs, and motivations.

■ DISC Assessment: Introduced in 1972 by industrial psychologist William Clark, the DISC assessment tool names the four types of behavior that demonstrate human emotion: dominance (D), influence (I), submission (S), and compliance (C). Clark's scheme, based on the 1928 research of lawyer and psychologist William Moulton Marston, asks participants to choose between two preferences from the

TIME TO SLOW DOWN AND REFLECT

YOUR PERSONALITY

CHILDHOOD MEMORIES

What memories associate with your personality?

How does your personality show in your memories?

When do your memories make you most happy?

CHILDHOOD INTERESTS

What did you love to do?

Where did you love to go?

Who did you love to be with?

CHILDHOOD DISLIKES

What activities did you strongly dislike?

Have your likes and dislikes changed?

What did you do because you had to?

list of four. Today, there are 160 behavioral patterns that can be identified from taking the DISC, all of which can help you better understand why you do what you do.

■ The Big Five: Sometimes referred to as the Five-Factor Model, this analytical tool is the result of the combined efforts of many researchers. It places these five traits in order of dominance for each individual: openness to experience, conscientiousness, extroversion, agreeableness, and neuroticism.

Originally conceived to find the correlation between personality and academic behavior, this tool is now used in a variety of ways, including predicting work behavior and burnout, indicating mental health disorders, and identifying learning styles.

■ The Enneagram: The Enneagram is a personality typing model that dates back to the 4th century. The modern version was heavily influenced by Russian mystic and philosopher G. I. Guirdjieff, who identified nine personality types: reformer, helper, achiever, individualist, investigator, loyalist, enthusiast, challenger, and peacemaker.

In using the tool, participants are asked to determine their strongest roles by choosing between two answers for multiple questions. Each role is associated with a number of characteristics in categories such as basic fear, vice/passion, temptation, and ego fixation. This is a more complex tool, but well worth the effort for the results it offers.

It's worth taking the time to identify your strongest personality traits because they are integral to understanding who you are. See the Resource section for more information if you want to delve deeper into the results these tools can provide.

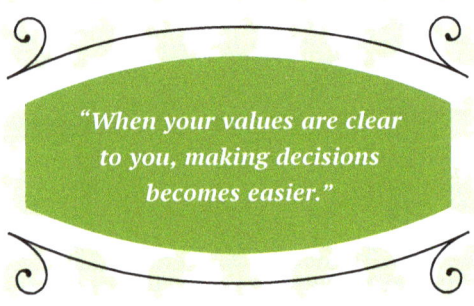

"When your values are clear to you, making decisions becomes easier."

EXPERIENCE

y mom asked, "Do you really need all those books?" as we struggled to fit everything in the car for our annual summer holiday to Barmouth, Wales. I was 11.

We stuffed the car with soda, tins of baked beans, and enough tea bags to last us a year. Even though our destination was less than three hours away, it looked like we were emigrating. I later learned it was a common belief that the Welsh increased prices for English tourists, so the huge amounts of groceries and dry goods were an effort to save money. I honestly didn't care as long as there was room for my books.

Neither of my parents were readers and placed little value on education, but my grandparents loved to read. My maternal grandfather was particularly curious. He never took anything at face value and always questioned what was presented as the truth.

Although I don't deny that genetics contributed to my love of learning, it was my early experiences and my wonderful nursery teacher, Mrs. Doors, that influenced me most heavily.

I loved Lane Head Nursery School from day one. My mom once told me how embarrassed she was on the first day of nursery school because I was the only who cried when it was time to go home time. I wanted to stay at school because I loved the lessons, especially the ones in theater, music, science, and art. The free-flowing and supportive environment made it acceptable for each of us to be unique.

After Lane Head Nursery, I went to Lodge Farm primary school, an open-plan (no classrooms) collaborative learning environment with wonderful teachers and lots of fun art and science projects. Then, when I was eight, we moved,

TIME TO SLOW DOWN AND REFLECT

YOUR EXPERIENCES

THE SET OF LIFE EXPERIENCES WE EACH POSSESS IS UNIQUE, AND EVERY ONE ADDS A LAYER TO WHO WE KNOW OURSELVES TO BE.

YOUR EXPERIENCES PLAY AS IMPORTANT A ROLE IN FINDING YOUR PASSION AS YOUR VALUES AND PERSONALITY.

How have your experiences shaped your values

?

Can you think of three experiences that have had a huge impact on you

?

What were the positives

?

What were the negatives

?

Where did having these experiences lead you

?

and I had to attend King Charles primary school.

Opened in the 1950s, King Charles was a very traditional school, with long tiled corridors leading to the classrooms. It was run by an old headmaster, Mr. Wilmot Brown, who forced us to attend morning assembly where we sat cross-legged, listening to rules and other announcements until it was time to stand and sing hymns.

The learning style at King Charles was much more structured than what I was used to. We learned the times tables by rote and read long passages that were followed by comprehension questions.

Then there were the handwriting lessons. Mrs. Jelfs, who taught both handwriting and science, insisted that everyone write with a fountain pen. We were all given cheap plastic fountain pens with small cartridges. I never could seem to regulate the pressure on the nib correctly, and the ink would splatter everywhere!

I didn't enjoy any of those things, but I loved science, particularly the experiments. One day, we were partnered up to do an experiment about floating and sinking. I had done similar projects at Lodge Farm, so I did my own work. When I was finished, I let my partner and a couple of other children copy some of my answers on their worksheets. When we got the results back, my work partner and the others who copied from me got As, but I didn't. Why? Because Mrs. Jelfs deducted points for ink splotches and not underlining properly.

This experience taught me at an early age that grades do not always reflect intelligence or understanding. As a result, I have pursued interests throughout my life without worrying about how to get good grades, but rather with a focus on learning about what is interesting.

> *"The decisions you make are a choice of values that reflect your life in every way."*

VALUES: FROM THE BEGINNING

I was fortunate to grow up in a family that valued happiness and togetherness. We shared meals with each other at the end of every day, and every summer we travelled to the same vacation spot in Barmouth in North Wales, where we met up with the extended family of aunts, uncles, and cousins. Perhaps it was this foundation that supported my love of adventure. I headed off any chance I got, sanctioned or not, to find the pot of gold at the end of the rainbow.

When I was 11, my friends and I found out that singer Kylie Minogue was going to be at the BBC Pebble Mill Studio in Birmingham. We took two buses and a train to get there, and skipped school just to get a peek at her. We ended up on the evening news chasing her limo. That night, my dad was reading the paper while the news was on, so he didn't see it. But the kids in school did, and we were all pretty famous for a while.

I still can't believe we never got caught, and the adventure brought me great joy. But it was another childhood experience that showed me one of my strongest values. I was in Germany in 1990 on a school trip. We were walking through Koln when I noticed a homeless family. They were obviously hungry, and their young daughter shivered from the cold. My friends continued on to the Cologne Cathedral while I found a store and bought bread and a coat for their daughter. They were appreciative, but I felt helpless. Wasn't there something else I could do?

I was a 14-year-old on a school trip and could not get my head around children begging on the streets. I had seen beggars before, of course. In my home town of Walsall, in the West Midlands of England, there would often be home-

> "...the core values that underpin sustainable development—interdependence, empathy, equity, personal responsibility and intergenerational justice—are the only foundation upon which any viable vision of a better world can possibly be constructed."

less drug addicts and alcoholics sitting in the town center. They were usually old men, and occasionally old women or young men. But never sober women and children.

I had never thought about my values, but I instinctively knew that this was wrong. It was not something that should happen in the world. I took action, without much thought, to provide something, even if it was only a little food and warmth. I left wishing I could do more, but I felt confident with all the other people passing that someone with more resources than I had would offer to help.

Dozens of people walked past this family, and no one even seemed to notice. Although this happened more than 25 years ago, all I need to do is close my eyes and the horror I felt still washes over me today. How could people be so cold? So uncaring?

In my 30s, I lived in San Francisco. On my way to work, I'd stroll along the Embarcadero—the beautiful seawall that parallels the San Francisco Bay—and found myself walking right past many people in need. The voice inside my head told me I certainly could not help every homeless person I passed, so why bother? To be honest, some of them scared me, and others disgusted me.

Seeing this reality on a daily basis was too much for me. It was easier to ignore, to stay focused on my own business, think about a new audio book, or plan out my day instead of stopping to connect. Ironically, I had become one of the desensitized people that I judged so harshly as a girl. It caused a lot of internal conflict because my values of equality and compassion had not changed.

I still cared about people but was overwhelmed with the need. After sitting in the discomfort for a while, I took advantage of the opportunity to join the board of Conard House, a local nonprofit organization with a mission to em-

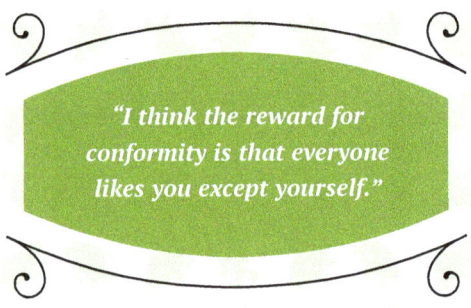

"I think the reward for conformity is that everyone likes you except yourself."

power those who live and work on the margins of society. In this organization, I found a more comfortable way to express my values. When I learned the history of the organization, I understood why.

Elaine Mikels, one of the founders of Conard House, believed that everyone deserved a place where they felt they belonged, a place they could call home. Her values came from her own sense of alienation and not belonging in the world, feelings that were rooted in her childhood.

In 1933, at the tender age of 12, Elaine began developing crushes on girls—quite a bewildering sensation, I would imagine. There was no understanding of sexual orientation at that time. Elaine's confusion manifested in ways that perplexed her Jewish mother, who sent her high-spirited tomboy daughter to a Catholic boarding school in the hope that it would straighten her out. Contrary to her mother's wishes, the love and attention Elaine experienced there instilled a strong sense of self, encouraging an even more independent spirit.

Like many closeted women during that time, Elaine had little construct to help her understand her sexuality, yet she still experienced the discomfort of living in a society where she felt different. Not quite able to conform, and still not ready to completely own who she was, Elaine lived at the edge of society, in a limbo of sorts that was neither welcoming nor comfortable. This experience came with a price that included depression, hospitalizations, and even expulsion by the State Department, where she was a relief worker in post-war Germany.

Although Elaine didn't feel strong enough to break out of the norm, she wandered through the 1950s, traveling the world. In her 1994 book, *Just Lucky I Guess: From Closet Lesbian to Radical Dyke*, she describes herself at that time

TIME TO SLOW DOWN AND REFLECT

YOUR VALUES

THINK ABOUT YOUR PERSONAL AND PROFESSIONAL LIFE

What was your happiest time

?

Where were you

?

Who were you with

?

What contributed to your happiness

?

How did you contribute to the happiness of others

?

What made you feel proud

?

Were there others who shared your pride

?

What factors helped you feel this way

?

as an "apolitical conformist."

In 1959, Elaine learned that a large number of mentally ill people returning to San Francisco from Napa State Hospital were in need of transitional services. Armed with a degree in social work from Berkeley, she bought a large Victorian home and created Conard House, the first halfway house in San Francisco. Through honoring her early value of belonging, she created an organization that today serves 1,600 people every year, supporting them and empowering them to be active participants in their community.

Despite the difficulties of coming to terms with her own background, Elaine Mikels found a way to express herself through her values, ultimately creating comfort and happiness for herself and others.

IDENTIFYING YOUR VALUES

here are many ways to figure out what you value. From secular to spiritual, they all require you to take the time to contemplate what's important to you.

Philosophers like Plato understood the significance of identifying and labeling values: In *The Republic Book IV*, he named prudence, justice, temperance, and courage as the core virtues necessary for a good life. More than 2,000 years later, in 1943, psychologist Abraham Maslow offered his Hierarchy of Needs, along with a concept he labeled "self-actualization." Maslow posited that values such as simplicity, beauty, and aliveness were necessary to realize one's talents and potential.

Over the centuries, many others have established lists of values, including social psychologist and cross-cultural researcher Shalom H. Schwartz, who developed the Universal Theory of Human Values, which crosses cultural boundaries. Schwartz's theory includes the values of self-direction, power, security, and conformity. Psychologist

TIME TO SLOW DOWN AND REFLECT

YOUR VALUES

Which 5 values would have been most important to you when you were very young ?

Which 5 became most important as you grew up ?

Which 5 seem most important to you today ?

CHOOSE FROM THIS LIST, OR COME UP WITH YOUR OWN.

- AUTHENTICITY
- ACHIEVEMENT
- ADVENTURE
- AUTHORITY
- AUTONOMY
- BALANCE
- BEAUTY
- BOLDNESS
- COLLABORATION
- COMPASSION
- COMPETITION
- CONNECTION
- CHALLENGE
- CITIZENSHIP
- COMMUNITY
- COMPETENCY
- CONTRIBUTION
- CREATIVITY
- CURIOSITY
- DETERMINATION
- EMPATHY
- FAITH
- FRIENDSHIP
- FAIRNESS
- FAME
- FUN
- GROWTH
- HAPPINESS
- HEALTH
- HONESTY
- HUMOR
- INFLUENCE
- INTEGRITY
- INNER HARMONY
- JUSTICE
- KINDNESS
- KNOWLEDGE
- LEADERSHIP
- LEARNING
- LOVE
- LOYALTY
- MEANINGFUL WORK
- OPENNESS
- PLEASURE
- POISE
- OPTIMISM
- PEACE
- POPULARITY
- RECIPROCITY
- RECOGNITION
- RELIGION
- REPUTATION
- RESPECT
- RESPONSIBILITY
- SECURITY
- SELF-RESPECT
- SERVICE
- SPIRITUALITY
- STABILITY
- SUCCESS
- STATUS
- TRUST
- WEALTH
- WISDOM

Jonathan Haidt included fairness and reciprocity.

The Ohio-based VIA Institute on Character, a nonprofit organization rooted in social psychology, has a free online tool (see Resource section) that helps determine key character strengths based on 24 core values. The list, which falls into six categories, borrows strongly from Plato's virtues; on it, you'll find creativity, bravery, kindness, and social intelligence.

Many of these secular lists possess conflicting values (Schwartz lists both conformity and self-direction, for instance), and you will certainly find similar conflicts in spiritual traditions. That's because it's all about balance.

For many spiritual traditions, there is an understanding that concepts like yin and yang aren't enemies. They both work in harmony to create balance. Traditions like Hinduism, for example, value both creation and destruction. In this system, the gods Brahma, the creator, and Shiva, the destroyer/transformer, are worshipped equally. Even Aristotle's work on values, which added to the work of Plato, determined that good values are established through finding a balance between extremes. Although it's deemed a virtue to have temperance, and insensibility and self-indulgence are both considered vices, a well-rounded life is achieved with balance.

VALUES UNDER STRESS

In a perfect world, we would all be able to maintain our integrity within the values we've come to know. But the world isn't perfect. Stressors that occur every day have the power to move us away from those values if we're not anchored in the knowledge of who we are and what's important to us. Even when you're aware, it can be difficult to stay aligned when your buttons are pushed.

One evening, after planning an appreciation party for the

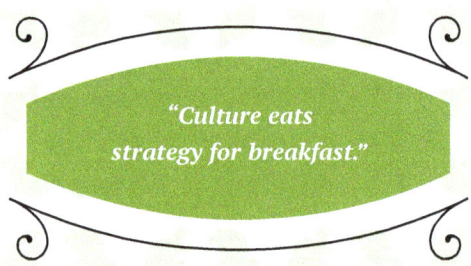

"Culture eats strategy for breakfast."

members and volunteers at a senior village where I once worked, I headed out to go home. As I stood at the bus stop with a smile on my face, caught up in the reverie of celebration, two teenage boys shot past me. On their way, one grabbed my cellphone right out of my hands. My feelings of joy and satisfaction quickly turned to anger and frustration as I spent my evening filing police reports and changing a ridiculous number of passwords.

That day, it was more than a challenge to hold onto my values of kindness, compassion, and respect. I wanted their heads on a platter! My strengths-based way of looking at the world had vanished and my Myers-Briggs personality of introvert/intuition/feeling/perceiving had morphed into traits I hardly recognized.

In the wake of this unexpected incident, I had to work very hard to communicate effectively. It was a challenge to make sure my feelings didn't override logic. And it wasn't long before intuition went out the window and judgment flew in, because under extreme stress, my dominant mode of perception got shut off and I became judgmental and critical. Suddenly, I was not open or empathetic.

There are two things that ultimately helped me find balance in that situation. First was my own awareness. I knew what my values were. Even though I was emotional, I was able to see how I wanted to toss those values aside, while also managing the feelings of justification that told me it was acceptable to do so.

Second, I had a safe place to process my feelings. At home, with a partner who let me get angry and express how I wanted those boys to be punished—imagining everything from medieval torture to posting photos at the bus shelters to warn others—I was able to move through the emotions more quickly. The insanity of the punishments I proposed

TIME TO SLOW DOWN AND REFLECT

YOUR VALUES UNDER STRESS

IT'S IMPORTANT TO LOOK INWARD, AND NOT JUST ABSORB THE VALUES OF THOSE AROUND YOU, AND TO THINK ABOUT THE IMPACT OF THE ACTIONS YOU TAKE AND HOW THEY WILL AFFECT OTHERS.

TRIGGERS

Who and what triggers your stress?

When and where is your stress triggered?

Why is your stress triggered?

REACTIONS

How do you react to stress?

What actions do you take?

What values do you demonstrate under stress?

OUTCOMES

What outcomes do you experience with stress?

What would you like to do differently?

How can you hold on to what's important to you?

allowed for humor and dissipated my anger. It was like releasing the steam from a pressure cooker so I could think and act in a way that was more aligned with my values. Negative experiences can have major impacts if we don't have a strong sense of what our own core values are.

THE IMPORTANCE OF KNOWING YOUR TEAM MEMBERS

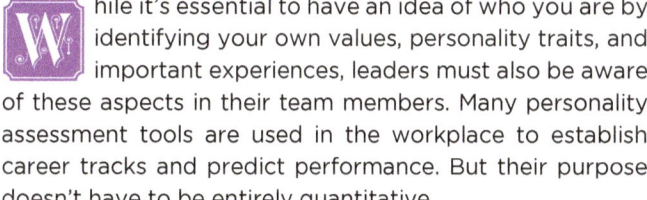hile it's essential to have an idea of who you are by identifying your own values, personality traits, and important experiences, leaders must also be aware of these aspects in their team members. Many personality assessment tools are used in the workplace to establish career tracks and predict performance. But their purpose doesn't have to be entirely quantitative.

As a young manager I once supervised a 17-year-old who worked for the company as a birthday party coordinator. She worked mainly on the weekend, so I usually communicated with her by phone and email. She was wonderful, and most of the time I heard glowing reviews. A few times, however, I got terrible feedback. "She was miserable. She did not engage with the children. Unhelpful."

When this happened, I couldn't believe this was the same girl I'd hired. She was smart, outgoing, warm, and positive. I would meet with her to find out what happened and she would tell me everything was fine, just that the parents were difficult. Then one day she didn't turn up for work.

Several months later, I received a letter. She had finally turned 18 and moved to Australia with her boyfriend. She was afraid her parents were going to take her to Pakistan and force her to get married. I never heard from her again.

I had no idea about what she was going through and wish I'd spent more time to learn about the challenges she was facing.

> *"As you live your values,
> your sense of identity, integrity,
> control, and inner-directedness
> will infuse you with both
> exhilaration and peace."*

I had no idea such a thing could happen in San Francisco. Child brides and forced marriages are still common in many parts of the world, but it wasn't a part of my world.

If I'd known her Myers-Briggs type, maybe I could have recognized that she was under severe stress. Taking the time to know and understand her experiences and values might have changed things. At the very least, it might have provided her with an opportunity to explore her decision before taking such drastic action.

As a leader, getting a feel for the values, personality traits, and experiences of your team members can help you utilize the best of what each has to offer. Recognizing the diversity of their strengths, and how an individual's qualitites might combine within a team, can be an asset. That knowledge can also help you know which communication style is most effective, choose the most inspiring motivational tools, and offer the most satisfying rewards for a job well done. The qualitative use of assessment tools can improve the quality of the team environment and nurture positive morale.

VALUES IN AN ORGANIZATION

Most organizations establish their values and make them part of their public "personas." We've all seen them—on their websites, marketing brochures, and annual reports. In understanding the true values of any organization, however, it's vital to assess whether those values are merely on display in the lobby, or if they actually guide everyday actions, including the stories that are told and the traditions they perpetuate. Sometimes the values on display are very different from the ones that are lived.

For example, here are the values promoted by Enron in its year 2000 annual report to shareholders:

TIME TO SLOW DOWN AND REFLECT

ORGANIZATIONAL VALUES

THINK ABOUT AN ORGANIZATION YOU WORK IN OR HAVE WORKED IN

Do you know its values

?

Are they the same or different from the ones presented to the public

?

Do they align with your personal values

?

Is the organization staying true to its values

?

Should you be working in a place that better aligns with your values

?

Should you start your own organization where you can stay true to your values and make a great impact on the world

?

- Communication: We have an obligation to communicate
- Respect: We treat others as we would like to be treated
- Integrity: We work with customers and prospects openly, honestly, and sincerely
- Excellence: We are satisfied with nothing less than the very best in everything we do

Enron filed for bankruptcy on December 2, 2001, and it was revealed that much of $111 billion in revenues was smoke and mirrors, the result of accounting fraud. For over a decade, the leaders of the organization had been purposely misrepresenting its financial health.

When the values on public display are so different from the ones demonstrated by action, it's easy to give up on them. Once you do, though, it can take a long time for an organization to return to them. Often times, the values become something else completely, and then, so does the organization.

Core values should not change over time. They should be fixed in both time and circumstance, and play an important role in how the organization confronts problems and makes decisions. They should serve as a guide for the organization in terms of principles and ethics.

Conard House, for example, has a strong, clear set of values that guide it to empower those that live on the margins of society. Just like the values of founder Elaine Mikels, the core values are unified by shared beliefs in individual worth, self-determination, personal responsibility, and social justice.

Strong founders can instill values that last for generations after they've gone. For example, physicist and educator Frank Oppenheimer, founder of San Francisco's Exploratorium, was adamant about the museum staying true to its values and principles. As a startup nonprofit in the late 1960s, they scrambled for funds, but never allowed their financial needs to compromise their values.

> "The CEO is not in charge of the company. The values are. If, at the end of our careers, we have not passed along positive values, we have abdicated our leadership role."

Still, those values were constantly tested. There is a great illustration of this, captured in the 1982 NOVA film *Palace of Delights*, when an argument took place between the Exploratorium's fundraising team and artist Bob Miller, who was an assistant director at the time. The fundraising crew wanted to rent out the museum to a local bank for a hefty fee, but the bank required that the Explainers (the museum's high-school-aged docents) be dressed a particular way.

Since the Exploratorium considers itself an institution based on teaching people how to think, not what to think, there was much debate about whether it was more important to get the money from the bank or let the Explainers decide for themselves what being "dressed up" meant. The fundraisers were perplexed that, in a time of financial crisis, Bob would argue that it was better not to book the event than allow the bank to dictate how their employees should dress.

"That's not very businesslike," the fundraising director accused.

"We're not a business," Bob responded. (Of course, the fundraisers argued that they were—after all, they were a licensed 501c3 and incorporated.)

"As important as it is to raise money for this place to keep it alive, we are not a business," Bob insisted. "The purpose of this place is to build a very good science education museum and those are two very different things."

At about this point in the conversation, the museum's founding director, Frank Oppenheimer, walked in. After listening for a moment, he interjected: "Just think how much nicer it would have been if someone had said to the Explainers, 'We want you to look nice, and now figure out how to do it,' and they could have come to an agreement

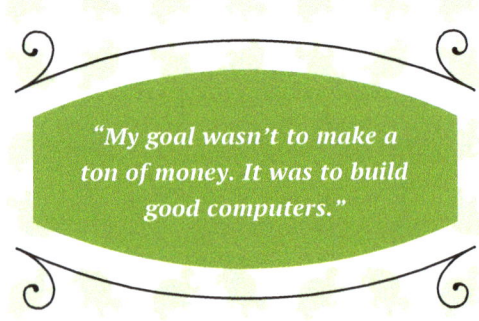

"My goal wasn't to make a ton of money. It was to build good computers."

themselves. I think that would have been a nice way to do it, and the way we should do it still." The fundraising person at first agreed, then followed with a "But...," to which Frank answered, "Well then, let's do it. Let's do it the nicer way."

The discussion went on for a bit more before the fundraising person, looking incredulous, says, "That might be the nicer way for the Explainers and us, but is it the nicer way for an important client? Do you care about that?" Again, Frank defended his position, explaining that just because someone is paying for it doesn't mean the organization has to do things they don't think are right.

"Even if it jeopardizes funds?" the fundraising person asks.

"Even if it jeopardizes funds," Frank responds, and then he adds, "Christ, we've jeopardized a lot of funds because we are so funny!"

Everyone laughs, including the fundraising person, who finally gives in and agrees to allow the Explainers to decide what being "dressed up" means to them.

This is such a great lesson for nonprofit—or, as I prefer to call them, "for-good"—organizations, especially those working in business development, marketing, and fundraising. You have to make it your job to understand the values of the organization and take a stand for those values when the time comes, on both the small and large issues. Compromising on the small things undermines the whole. Strong organizations live by their core values, even if those values sometimes become a competitive disadvantage; even if it means turning down short-term profits.

An organization's values are just as important as personal ones, and can easily be compromised in difficult and stressful times. This can bring even the best of organiza-

> *"Your personal core values define who you are, and a company's core values ultimately define the company's character and brand. For individuals, character is destiny. For organizations, culture is destiny."*

tions to a crossroads; often, the real values that people are expressing are miles away from the ones the public sees. As I experienced when my phone was stolen, the right choices are made when you are aware of what your values are. Once you have a benchmark with which to compare options and potential outcomes, it becomes clear whether or not a decision is aligned with your values. Your choices become conscious ones, not ones made from fear or from desperation.

It's also important to have a safe space to "vent," at work as well as at home—a place to blow off the steam of anger, frustration, and confusion, for both leaders and team members. In fact, part of being a leader is curating a team of confidants and advisors who will allow you to speak in a stream of consciousness. A strong team will understand that your reaction to a stressful situation is just part of a process that can get you back on track, and put you in a place where you can take action that is in line with your core values.

My time at the Exploratorium began many years after Dr. Frank Oppenheimer had died. There were no core values hanging on the wall, yet Frank's values and principles were still strong and shared throughout the organization. I understood them even before I knew what they were.

WHEN VALUES CLASH

In 1986, when Larry Harvey and his friend Jerry James celebrated the summer solstice at Baker Beach Park in San Francisco with a bonfire, they upheld a tradition started by Mary Grauberger several years earlier, but with one fundamental difference: They created a giant wooden sculpture of a man nine feet tall, and another smaller sculpture of a dog; then they burned both in effigy. Harvey says it was a spontaneous "act of radical expression."

"An empowered organization is one in which individuals have the knowledge, skill, desire, and opportunity to personally succeed in a way that leads to collective organizational success."

This was the beginning of what is known as Burning Man, a month-long event in Nevada's Black Rock Desert that now requires construction of a temporary city to house everyone who attends. The 2016 crowd was estimated at 70,000. Each year, people from all over the world come together there to celebrate art and expression.

As with any organization, the festival has had its growing pains. In the early 1990s, several groups—most famously the Cacophony Society, self-described "random eccentrics"—began to participate. Each group arrived in the desert, bringing beautiful fragments to contribute to the whole. But the more people who joined in, the more chaos occurred. Although the founders were anarchists by nature, rules became necessary and factions began to form.

"During our early history in the desert, in the mid-90s, there was a lot of infighting about what the event was for," says Harvey. "That struggle culminated in 1996. It concerned what our city was for, and who the entire event belonged to."

Larry Harvey was passionate about keeping Burning Man true to its original values of bringing people together on an equal playing field to find community through art, expression, discussion, and reliance—no matter how large it grew (see the Resource section for links to more information). In 2004, he created the festival's 10 Principles, not to control participants' actions, but rather to reflect the community's culture and philosophy. The first on the list is "Radical Inclusion," defined like this: "Anyone may be a part of Burning Man. We welcome and respect the stranger. No prerequisites exist for participation in our community."

During the 2016 Burning Man event, however, that principle was questioned, and those who felt it wasn't being upheld by one of the camps, called White Ocean, took action. The White

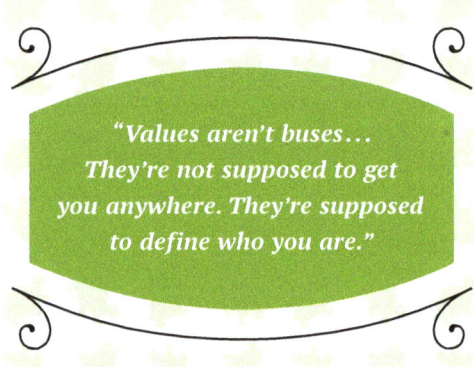

*"Values aren't buses…
They're not supposed to get
you anywhere. They're supposed
to define who you are."*

Ocean camp was begun three years before by the son of a Russian billionaire and a well-known DJ from England. The founders claimed the purpose of their enclave was to unite people through music. They invited dozens of internationally known DJs to stay in their camp and spin records for all who wanted to listen and dance.

Some of the other festival-goers saw it a little differently. They felt the camp and its founders only wanted to make Burning Man the "place" to be seen, that it was a luxurious and ultra-exclusive display meant to be photographed and shared on social media. They asserted that VIP access and separate lodging and food venues for the DJs created an elitist atmosphere that did not uphold the festival's principle of radical inclusion, and started a "revolution against rich parasites."

The war cry began when the power lines to the White Ocean camp were cut and the site was flooded with water. Trailer doors were glued shut, causing complete mayhem. The camp organizers were outraged and could not understand why they had been targeted, even though White Ocean had violated many of the principles of the festival.

Of course, the vandals did not abide by Burning Man values either, which included operating in accordance with local, state, and federal laws. And their behavior wasn't exactly inclusive either. Nonetheless, this is what can happen when the values or principles of an organization are not anchored within everyone involved.

This may seem like an extreme example, and in some ways it is. The festival is still guided and "scripted" by Harvey, but with 70,000 people in attendance, how much structure can there really be? At the same time, it's a cautionary tale. When some people within an organization feel that the importance of "walking the walk" has disappeared, extreme action is a potential outcome. This story does demonstrate, however,

> "Enlightened leadership is spiritual if we understand spirituality not as some kind of religious dogma or ideology, but as the domain of awareness where we experience values like truth, goodness, beauty, love, and compassion, and also intuition, creativity, insight, and focused attention."

that like personal values, an organization's values can also be easily compromised in difficult and stressful times.

Choices can only be aligned with values—both personally and professionally—when they're instilled within the members of an organization. If your personal values don't align with the values of the organization where you work, there may be better solutions for you elsewhere.

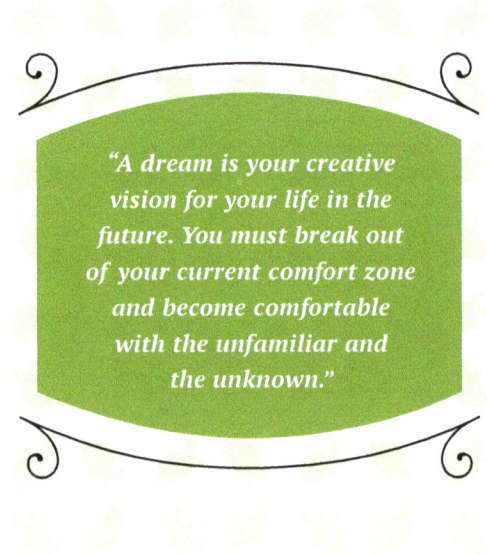

"A dream is your creative vision for your life in the future. You must break out of your current comfort zone and become comfortable with the unfamiliar and the unknown."

CHAPTER FOUR
Paint Your Future
What does your future look like?

YOUR LIFE IS LIMITED BY YOUR THINKING

y very first job was working in a cake shop at age 11. I loved computer games and going out, so I got a job. I earned £10 (about $18) for a whole Saturday.

At 14, I began working as a waitress at a local hotel. At that time, in my hometown of Walsall, in the West Midlands of England, waitresses didn't get tips, and we had no busboys to help. We did it all for £3, about $5.40 per hour.

I worked there for four years, until I left for university. I did not enjoy one minute of it. I didn't like the way my clothes smelled from the kitchen after a long shift, and I didn't like the boring, repetitive work, setting the tables or refilling the salt and pepper shakers. But what I hated most was waiting on people. I didn't mind taking orders if the people were nice, but I hated bringing the food to the table and clearing away the dishes.

Because Walsall is an industrial town, we saw very few tourists. There was only one attraction in town: the Arboretum, a big park where the highlight was the winter light display. Unfortunately, many of the lights were old and

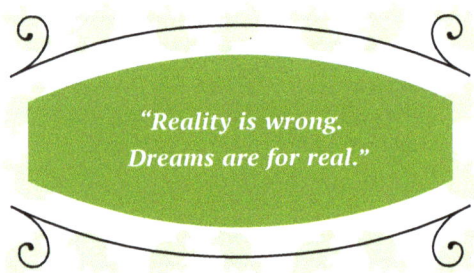

*"Reality is wrong.
Dreams are for real."*

couldn't compare with the famous holiday light display in Blackpool, a seaside town a few hours away.

Most of the guests at the hotel where I worked were there on business, or in town for a family event, like a wedding. Sometimes, on a Saturday, I would get a large coach group. This could mean only one thing: another group of suckers had signed up for a "Mystery Tour."

"You've got to be joking," they would say. "What a dump. No wonder they call this a mystery tour. It's the only way they get people here." They were usually in a horrible mood and complained about everything, wishing they were eating fish and chips by the seaside.

At this young age, I didn't know what I wanted to do when I grew up. All I knew was I didn't want to live in Walsall. I wanted to travel and have people wait on me, not the other way round. So I worked hard and moved to Southern England, then on to Northern England, then London, Munich, and eventually San Francisco. With a good education and strong work ethic, I found myself in fun jobs that allowed me to have the lifestyle I wanted.

It was more than I could ever have imagined while stacking salad bowls in that Walsall hotel. I wonder, however, if my choices would have been different had I received the advice entrepreneur Tim Ferriss gives: "Think big and don't listen to people who tell you it can't be done. Life is too short to think small."

My mom just wanted me to be happy, and my dad could find fun in the most mundane work. He had the gift of gab and worked in his own shop all his life. Never taking life too seriously, he reveled in making small talk with local customers. He always found the silver lining and the joke in situations. "You've gotta have a loff," he would say, chuckling to himself.

"Big thinking precedes great achievement."

While I appreciate the lack of pressure that came from my parents, and the value they placed on being happy, I don't know who I might have become if I'd been encouraged to dream bigger. Yes, they taught me that enjoying life was important. But they also communicated—even if not in so many words—that the goal was to make the best of situations that weren't ideal, rather than to go out and create better situations. Whether at home or at work, this survival mechanism never serves us as humans, nor does it offer support to organizations that consider themselves to be "for good."

Thinking small can be an enormous hindrance. Short-term, or survival thinking ("What do I need right now?") is rarely the best way to move forward. In an interview with marine biologist Sylvia Earle, anthropologist Jane Goodall explains how the drive for instant gratification has mitigated the importance of viewing things in the long term. She discusses how Native Americans used to make decisions only after asking "How will it affect our people…generations to come?" Now we ask, "How will it affect the next shareholder meeting?" or "How will it affect me now?"

"It makes me ashamed of my species," Goodall says. "It makes me angry, but it makes me more determined to carry on doing what I am doing. It makes me work harder because the older we get, the less time we have."

Once you've identified your values, having considered what you care about and what's important, you can begin to paint a picture for yourself and others to see. You become a changemaker. As the details of your life change, you add to the picture, but the essence remains the same. It empowers you to know you're on the right path, gaining knowledge and building skills to reach for bigger goals and create better lives, organizations, and communities.

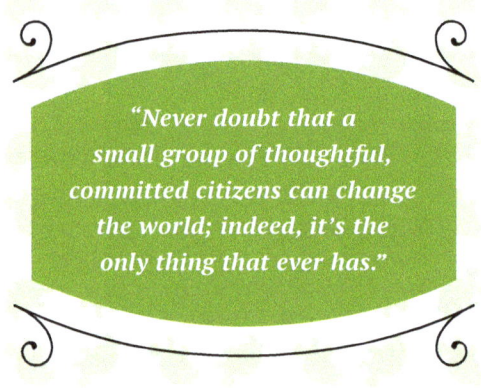

"Never doubt that a small group of thoughtful, committed citizens can change the world; indeed, it's the only thing that ever has."

VISION AND VALUES

ou've already expended a good amount of energy discovering your values—those qualities that are of the utmost importance to you. It's essential to have a strong foundation for your own set of principles before you start to create any vision, whether it's for yourself or for an organization.

Having a vision is essential for successful and sustainable change. A clear vision empowers you to create that which you really want. To be effective, the vision needs to be future oriented, compelling, aspirational, and bold.

George Cadbury, founder of the Cadbury cocoa and chocolate company, is one of my favorite businessmen and philanthropists because he successfully wove together his values and vision. As a Quaker, he valued equality and integrity, something most 19th-century industrialists did not consider to be important. In his 1923 book *The Life of George Cadbury*, author A.G. Gardiner compares Cadbury to Tolstoy. There is, however, one very important distinction in how each of these men reacted to the reality of the times in which they lived.

Gardiner relates that when Tolstoy was brought face to face with the horrors in the lives of the Moscow poor, he broke into sobs and cried out, "How can these things be?" With scorn, Gardiner writes that Tolstoy "repudiated the whole machinery of society, and preached personal salvation as one escape from the monstrous toils in which humanity was caught."

Cadbury, on the other hand, "had a practical genius, which differentiated him." In Gardiner's estimation, while Cadbury was sensitive to the suffering and injustice in the world, he didn't reject civilization. He was aware of the "evils" attached to modern industry and how factory

> "But if each man could have his own house, a large garden to cultivate and healthy surroundings—then, I thought, there will be for them a better opportunity of a happy family life."

life affected the workers, but his dreams "always sprang from a businesslike acceptance of the facts and tendencies of life."

Cadbury understood that the system, with all its vagaries, was "essential to society as it existed." He realized that the vision wasn't rejecting or ignoring the current conditions, rather it was "humanizing the system and spiritualizing the social relationships of men."

"It is unreasonable," Cadbury said, "to expect a man to lead a healthy, holy life in a back street or a sunless slum." Gardiner wrote that Cadbury's values showed him that "human growth, like any other, must have light and air before it could develop its beauty and fragrance."

Because he married his values with his vision, one of Cadbury's biggest contributions was becoming a pioneer of the Garden City Movement, a style of urban planning that adds the splendor of nature to the concrete and stone of the city. Cadbury bought farmland nearly five miles from his original plant in Birmingham, England, and moved production there so his employees could be surrounded by nature and beauty. It was dubbed "the factory in the garden."

I grew up in a city house, not far from Birmingham, with a back garden at the rear of the property. So did all my friends, both rich and poor. All of our houses had a back bedroom with a window that looked out over that garden. As a child, I took this for granted, but the children growing up in Walsall, as in other towns of the industrial Black Country, had this gift due to the vision of George Cadbury and others like him.

Less than a century before, conditions for children had been very different. Some worked in mines and many labored in factories, carrying out the most dangerous jobs

TIPS
CREATING YOUR VISION BOARD

GATHER MATERIALS AHEAD OF TIME

Several pieces of sturdy paper or poster board
(11 x 17 or 22 x 28 inches are great sizes)

Tools and materials such as old magazines, colored paper, scissors, tape, and glue

Paints, crayons, pens in an array of weights and colors, and a frame for your final piece

ADD THOUGHTS AND IMAGES

Quotes that bring you joy and images that inspire you

Items from nature that make you feel good:
leaves, flower petals, wood

SET THE MOOD

Select some music—inspirational, energetic, dance

Choose an aroma—favorite candles, essences, flowers

Indulge your taste buds—rich chocolate, berries

PICK A DATE AHEAD OF TIME

Find a time when you'll be alone and uninterrupted

Work under a new or full moon to add atmosphere

Target a date that is meaningful to you

MAKE A COMMITMENT

Decide on how much time you're willing to spend every day and schedule it on your calendar

Put your vision board where you can see it every day

DO AN END RUN ON RESISTANCE

Be messy, spontaneous—go with your gut!

Pretend you're a child making a child's vision board

Do a speed vision board first:
give yourself just 5 or 10 minutes to complete

as they crawled under machinery to collect valuable materials that had fallen. All the sooty gray images of 19th-century industrial life did not deter Cadbury from envisioning his "factory in a garden." Bournville Village, which sits on the original property of Cadbury's factory, has restrictions to this day that support his vision of beauty.

With this model in mind comes the realization that we all can create a vision very different from the reality in which we live. Cadbury's ability to do so demonstrated through action that slum conditions, for instance, were not a necessity of the industrial system. In order for a new reality to be sustainable, however, vision must be aligned with values.

DREAMING YOUR FUTURE

There is a difference between daydreaming and dreaming. One is an escape. The other is a bridge to what you want. Building a bridge requires effort and thought. It's wonderful to have ideas about what you want to do and create, but fantasizing about them without taking action accomplishes nothing.

Sometimes it's hard to know where to start, especially if you haven't identified where your passion lies. Don't let that be an excuse. There are ways to jumpstart your future, and combining dreaming with action is one of them. Henri Breuil, a 20th-century French anthropologist and priest, studied prehistoric cave paintings for much of his career. He believed that one purpose of the cryptic glyphs was to serve as a "vision board" that people believed would manifest more animals for upcoming hunts. Some might say these were the original vision boards.

Today, everyone from popular *Chicken Soup for the Soul* author Jack Canfield and actor Jim Carey to superstars

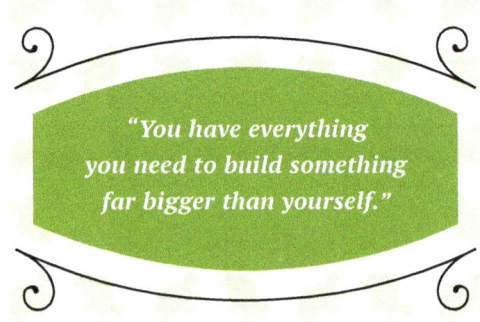

"You have everything you need to build something far bigger than yourself."

Ellen DeGeneres and Oprah have talked openly about their experiences using vision boards.

Then there is Lucinda Cross. As a college freshman, she made a bad decision that landed her in a federal penitentiary for four-and-a-half years. She didn't want to become a statistic, so while she was incarcerated, she created a vision board of her own. This choice was the seed that helped her grow a successful business that shows women how they can create a different life based on their own personal experiences. Today, Cross is widely considered an expert in personal and professional motivation, and has been interviewed in many publications, as well as on national TV.

Lucinda could have focused on the decision that imprisoned her. Instead, she focused on creating a life of "fire, fun, and freedom." And it all started with a vision board.

What exactly is a vision board? Very simply, it's whatever helps you to "see" the life that you imagine. You can make one using magazines, a glue stick, and poster board. By cutting out pictures and words that symbolize the achievements, experiences, and possessions you dream of, you can create a collage that can be placed near your work or sleeping space to inspire you.

There are no rules or limitations in making a vision board. However, there are a few guidelines that can help you to stay focused. First, don't use too many images; they can blur your true intention. Next, focus different sections of the board on specific topics—finances, career, personal life—but represent all aspects of your life on one board. Finally, remember that work/life balance is a misnomer. Everything you do affects everything else in your life.

Some may think this process sounds a bit esoteric, even "woo-woo." You may resist because you feel that it's not

> *"Glance at the sun.*
> *See the moon and the stars.*
> *Gaze at the beauty of*
> *Earth's greenings.*
> *Now, think."*

grounded in scientific principles, but never doubt the power of imagination! The point is to open a door so that what is inside can get out. A vision board is that door. You're taking what's in your imagination and bringing it into this world. Creating a vision board can help solidify the things that, right now, you only dream about. It can move you closer to manifesting those dreams.

Take your time to enjoy the experience. You never know what your subconscious is trying to communicate. If you focus on being "neat," you might actually be censoring yourself. Let yourself imagine what can be, and experience the wonder that accompanies seeing your vision come to life.

Once you've completed your vision board, spend time with it every day, feeling the emotions that the pictures and words stir up in you. Consider taking a photo of your board and using it as your screen saver or the lock window on your phone. This way, your goals and desires are in front of you every time you work or call someone. Every minute you spend with it can bring you one step closer to making it a reality.

ADDING STRATEGY

ow that you have a handle on your values, and at least the seed of a vision, let's turn to the practical, on-the-ground piece: strategy.

Adding strategy is different from labeling values or creating vision. Developing a strategy is about finding solutions, the means to achieve your vision. At its core, a strategy is "the way" to bring your vision to fruition. It's about making choices that align with your values and allocating the resources available to actually create the future you want.

"The future of any corporation is as good as the value system of the leaders and followers in the organization."

That's the simple definition. The actual development of a strategy is much more complex and even more intricate than what ends up in a written plan. It's more like a game of chess: You are in control of the moves you make, but you can't predict the moves made by others. A good strategist ponders the outcomes of outcomes, and the outcome of those outcomes, devising different options to navigate unforeseen circumstances.

In addition to creating a road map to define how problems will be solved, a strategy lays out in detail what needs to be lined up, both internally and externally, for you to succeed. In creating your strategy, you'll find a whole range of current and potential behaviors and activities to navigate. New roads and obstacles will be uncovered. You may even find that you knew about some of them on a subconscious level before you acknowledged them. In the process of creating your strategy, you'll learn how to trust your instincts. There will be plenty of opportunities for you to decide what's important. You may find yourself following a passion or paying attention to something that is calling to you, even if you don't know yet what it has to do with your long-term vision.

There is a difference between a strategic decision and an operational decision. Strategic decisions are about how to achieve long-term outcomes, not day-to-day functions. They can be very complex, and have many variable factors. You may not be able to predict accurate outcomes from strategic decisions. The circumstances and influences that are out of your control (competition, trends, illness, weather) mean that outcomes are likely to be uncertain, layered, and ill-defined. That's why, unlike your values, your strategy needs to be flexible. Even visions can be altered, but if your values change, then you are no longer the same person.

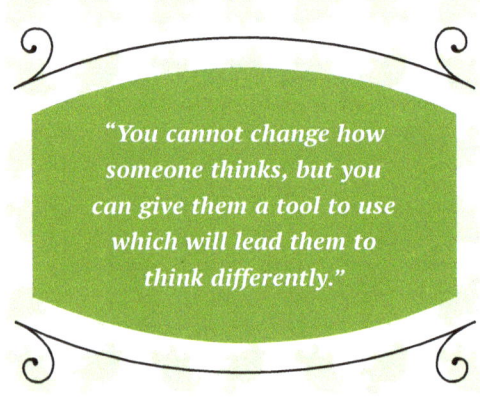

"You cannot change how someone thinks, but you can give them a tool to use which will lead them to think differently."

TOOLS FOR BUILDING STRATEGY

A good strategy can help you identify opportunities and places where you can take your vision. There are many tools available to help you lay a solid foundation for a successful strategy. I've offered a few here. Many professionals I know use tools like these, and I've seen how effective they can be when used in a way that is inclusive and focuses on vision. See the Resource section for more information

▪ SWOT Analysis: A SWOT analysis (Strengths, Weaknesses, Opportunities, and Threats) is a matrix of sorts that can be used by businesses, organizations, and even individuals. Specifying your objective (aka your vision), and then identifying internal and external factors that either support or thwart it, allows you to stay ahead of the game. Strengths and weaknesses are the internal factors; opportunities and threats are external.

▪ PEST Analysis: A PEST analysis (Political, Economic, Social, Technological) can help you identify and evaluate external factors that could affect your vision. This tool makes you aware of big-picture opportunities and threats you might not otherwise have thought about. It's vital to be aware of them in developing your strategy so you don't miss a huge opportunity or get caught off guard by something that could result in a setback.

▪ Gap Analysis: This tool is exactly what it sounds like: It helps you evaluate the differences between where you are and where you want to go. Using your vision as the destination and being honest about your current state allows you to create a road map of specific actions. When combined with the data culled from SWOT and PEST analyses, this information can speed up the time needed to achieve your vision.

TIPS
FOR USING STRATEGY TOOLS

GUIDELINES FOR GROUP SESSIONS

Be sure that all participants understand the categories and the purpose of the tool

Use an unbiased facilitator

Describe the brainstorming process in writing beforehand and verbally at the start

Establish rules ahead of time and communicate them to all participants

Include stakeholders who bring a variety of perspectives

Ask individuals to complete the tool on their own prior to any group discussion

Post a list of the rules in the meeting room

Allow more junior staff to go first to mitigate intimidation

Use a structured approach that incorporates a round-robin process

When in the brainstorming phase, keep generating ideas

Limit discussion on individual ideas until brainstorming is over

Break into small groups to discuss each category

Come back together to share small-group findings

Evaluate synergy between strategy, values, and vision

■ Blue Ocean Strategy: This is a newer tool, but one that is just as—if not more—valuable. Developed by W. Chan Kim and Renée Mauborgne, professors at INSEAD, an international graduate business school, this tool is predicated on the hypothesis that you don't succeed by battling competitors, but rather by creating "blue oceans" of new market space. By using the Blue Ocean Strategy, you or your organization can set strategic goals, plug your information into supporting models, or create competitor profiles.

Hopefully, one or more of the tools here can be of help in planning your strategy. In my own experience, however, when these strategy-developing tools are used in the workplace, they're sometimes carried out in ways that miss the mark. Use the tips on the facing page to avoid some common pitfalls.

VISION IS NEVER ABOUT MAKING MONEY

Traditionally, vision is defined as what the future looks like; strategy is defined as how you get there—how you plan to achieve the outcomes necessary to fulfill your vision. A large part of any organizational strategy is how it will sustain itself—planning how funds will be raised or revenue earned. Organizations have long used the process of planning and strategizing to turn profits.

Yes, money is a part of it. Without money, an organization can't stay alive. Strategies about profits, retaining employees, growing, and reducing risk are vital aspects to survival. The problem comes when no one asks the question, "At what cost are we profitable?" No amount of money is ever worth compromising your values.

Unfortunately, in times of economic downturn, or without a clear vision and strong guiding principles, even the best

> "We achieved our mission to the moon. Let's look home from that lofty perch and reimagine our mission on Earth—that is what we need to do here. Together, we can upcycle everything. The world will be better for our positive visions and actions."

for-good organizations can develop tunnel vision. They can begin to focus on meeting revenue goals and reducing expenses in the short-term, rather than retaining their vision for the long-term. Sometimes these measures can help, but other times they can signal impending derailment from an organization's values and vision. When these important tenets are forgotten, employees may start to think their sole purpose is to make money rather than to stand by founding principles.

It's important that for-good organizations remember that their purpose is not to make money. Changemakers need to know the cost they're willing to pay to be profitable. What arms and legs can be cut off to save heart and soul? If you don't have heart and soul, you are not a for-good organization.

There has been a for-good business model for nearly thirty years (remember the "Fourth Wave" organizations discussed in Chapter 1?). Today, as we approach the third decade of the 21st century, the time is ripe for those who see there is a different way to do things. But it takes a strong sense of knowing what you stand for, where you can be flexible and where you must stay true to your values. If you don't have awareness, you're not who you say you are, even if you keep the same name.

START SMALL AND DON'T FIGHT THE SYSTEM

Oceanographer Sylvia Earle's goal is to save "her baby," the beautiful blue ocean. There are many strategies she could have chosen, such as focusing on removing plastics or fighting pollution, but that's not the path she's taken.

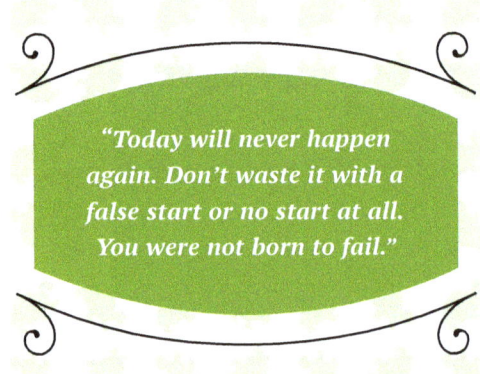

"Today will never happen again. Don't waste it with a false start or no start at all. You were not born to fail."

It's not that she doesn't support cleaning up the ocean, it's just that she's devised a better strategy—one that's more in line with her vision. She's focused on identifying key marine areas and protecting them so they remain rich and vibrant, ensuring that their goodness will extend to the whole ocean. Her work has established a new model, an innovative way to accomplish what others had been trying to do for years.

To build a world—one no longer driven by money-making mindsets and soul-sucking work—we have to create and nurture solid, for-good organizations that are so strong their goodness extends to the whole planet. This won't happen overnight. Sylvia Earle started with one location she called a "Hope Spot." Now, there are dozens. Sustainable change starts small.

I have a friend whose family opened a restaurant in the U.S. in the mid-1970s. It had been her grandfather's dream for years, and the excitement generated by finally seeing it on the verge of being realized blurred his vision.

He and his business partners got caught up in the excitement and enthusiasm, but no one was paying attention to the vision or establishing a thoughtful strategy to achieve it. They built an enormous facility, complete with banquet rooms and a lounge, and things went quite well...until the energy crisis hit.

Suddenly, the natural gas the restaurant needed was no longer as plentiful. In order to stay open, they had to heat over 10,000 square feet with propane, a much more expensive fuel. The added expense was more than they could handle. Within a year, they had to close their doors.

The impact was enormous—not just on the owners and the employees who lost their jobs, but on the community that had come to rely on them. Had they started smaller

TIME TO SLOW DOWN AND REFLECT

QUESTIONS TO PONDER

Who will your vision affect

?

How will your vision make the world better

?

What effect will it have on the environment

?

What effects will it have on animals

?

What effect will it have on people

?

What effect will it have on relationships

?

What long-term effect could it have on society

?

How will those in other countries or in the future be affected by your vision

?

and more cautiously, who knows how long they might have operated?

There's a lesson to be learned here: Don't let the excitement that inevitably accompanies identifying your values and creating your vision override the importance of taking your time to create a strategy. There's no need to go out and hire a consultant to conduct SWOT, PEST, and Gap analyses all at once. Pick one. Then select one category. Focus on a single aspect of that category.

Develop a reasonable timeline that allows people to breathe: space is essential for creativity to bloom. When you find yourself in an environment where the vision is unclear, or if people are moving in multiple directions, don't fight those who oppose you. Instead, plant seeds to work with those who are like-minded on projects that align with your vision.

The Cadbury chocolate empire we all know today started out in 1824 when George Cadbury's father, John, began selling coffee, tea, and drinking chocolate from a small shop in Birmingham, England. More than 20 years later, one of George's brothers, Benjamin (who had manufacturing experience), joined their father, and together the Cadburys built their first factory.

George and his other brother, Richard, took over the business in 1861, nearly 40 years after their father started it. They didn't move the business to the countryside until 1878, which is what led to the creation of Bournville, the model village where George Cadbury expressed his love of nature, appreciation for the environment, and commitment to creating a healthy, respected workforce.

George Cadbury's accomplishments started with the value of equality, passed down from his father through their Quaker beliefs. His vision was that of a profitable

> *"There is something patently insane about all the typewriters sleeping with all the beautiful plumbing in the beautiful office buildings, and all the people sleeping in the slums."*

business supported by workers who were surrounded by beauty, and who could grow as human beings and enjoy a life outside of a grimy city. This required strategy. And patience. Achieving that vision didn't happen overnight.

Find your patience. Discover ways to nurture your excitement while resisting the urge to achieve everything at one time. That's how legacies are built.

Peter Senge, a brilliant scientist who lectures at MIT, talks about growing up in the paradise that was Los Angeles in the 1950s. As a child, he and his family could drive for hours and see nothing but lemon and orange groves. In a decade, they were all gone, replaced by parking lots, housing developments, and shopping malls. The air was no longer clear or clean. He literally watched paradise disappear.

This experience has driven much of Senge's career. After watching the destruction of his boyhood home, Senge decided there was really just one problem in the world: interdependence. What he saw was a lack of understanding that everything we do affects everything else.

Senge posits that if people had been asked if they wanted polluted air that destroyed the groves, eliminated the possibility of kids walking to school, and playing safely outside, no one would've said, "Yes!" It was no one's vision to destroy paradise. People wouldn't have wanted that. But no one thought about the potential outcome.

Senge observes that while we have all become more interdependent, we've also become less aware of it, resulting in suffering for humans and living creatures which no one intended. Our interdependence has grown and our awareness of it has declined, leading to mass disconnection and suffering for humanity.

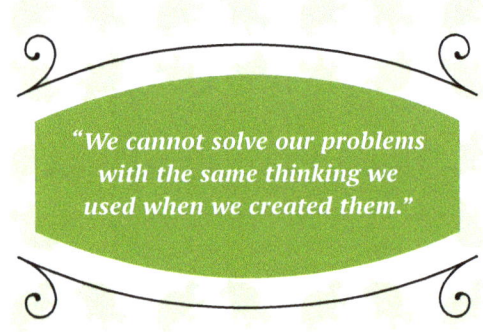

"We cannot solve our problems with the same thinking we used when we created them."

George Cadbury knew about interdependence long before Peter Senge was even born. He had an instinct to work with nature to improve the conditions of his workers because he understood the cycle of dependence: His workers depended on the beauty of nature to feel happy, and their happiness fostered a more successful community and work experience. Employing people who were appreciative and content increased productivity.

The Cadbury legacy is rooted in interdependence, a concept worth contemplating before you begin to form ideas about how to bring your own vision into reality. Think about how your vision fits within the world as a whole. Ask yourself if what you are doing will make the world a better place.

Chapter One

"Passion is one great force that unleashes creativity, because if you're passionate about something, then you're more willing to take risks."
CELLIST YO-YO MA
6

"Have the courage to follow your heart and intuition. They somehow already know what you truly want to become. Everything else is secondary."
COMPUTER VISIONARY STEVE JOBS
8

"I have no special talent. I am only passionately curious."
PHYSICIST ALBERT EINSTEIN
10

"Nothing is really work unless you would rather be doing something else."
SCOTTISH NOVELIST JAMES M. BARRIE
12

"Everything on Earth has a purpose, every disease an herb to cure it, and every person a mission. This is the Indian theory of existence."
NATIVE AMERICAN AUTHOR CHRISTAL QUINTASKET
16

"We typically think of the leader as being the person at the top. But if you define a leader as an executive, then you absolutely deny everyone else in an organization the opportunity to be a leader."
BUSINESS SYSTEMS EXPERT & EDUCATOR PETER SENGE
18

"Find out what you love. Do it because you love it. Stick with it. Start now."
INVENTOR NIKOLA TESLA
20

"I'd rather lose myself in passion than lose my passion."
AWARD-WINNING FRENCH DIVER JACQUES MAYOL
22

QUOTES
Chapter Two

"I sincerely believe that energy grows from itself and the more energy you expend the more you create within yourself. I also believe energy is a habit which can be created quite easily. In other words, use your energy and more energy flows, and then it is very hard to stop—as if one would ever want to!"
FASHION ICON DIANA VREELAND
26

"There is nothing so useless as doing efficiently that which should not be done at all."
MANAGEMENT CONSULTANT PETER F. DRUCKER
28

"Treating people the same is not equal treatment if they are not the same."
LINGUISTICS PROFESSOR DEBORAH TANNEN
30

"We want to take action out of the desire to contribute to life rather than out of fear, guilt, shame, or obligation."
PSYCHOLOGIST MARSHALL B. ROSENBERG
32

"People are born with intrinsic motivation, self-esteem, dignity, curiosity to learn, joy in learning."
MANAGEMENT LEADER W. EDWARDS DEMING
34

"Control leads to compliance; autonomy leads to engagement."
BUSINESS AUTHOR DANIEL H. PINK
36

"If you treat an individual as he is, he will remain how he is. But if you treat him as if he were what he ought to be and could be, he will become what he ought to be and could be."
**DIPLOMAT & PHILOSOPHER
JOHANN WOLFGANG VON GOETHE**
38

"Be strong enough to stand alone, be yourself enough to stand apart, but be wise enough to stand together when the time comes."
AUTHOR & POET MARK AMEND
44

"The happiness of a man in this life does not consist in the absence but in the mastery of his passions."
POET ALFRED LORD TENNYSON
50

"Connection is the energy that is created between people when they feel seen, heard, and valued—when they can give and receive without judgment."
SOCIAL SCHOLAR & STORYTELLER BRENÉ BROWN
52

"One can choose to go back toward safety or forward toward growth. Growth must be chosen again and again; fear must be overcome again and again."
PSYCHOLOGIST ABRAHAM H. MASLOW
54

"Start by doing what's necessary, then do what's possible, and suddenly you are doing the impossible."
SAINT FRANCIS OF ASSISI
56

QUOTES
Chapter Three

"To be yourself in a world that is constantly trying to make you something else is the greatest accomplishment."
ESSAYIST & POET RALPH WALDO EMERSON
58

"Authentic values are those by which a life can be lived, which can form a people that produces great deeds and thoughts."
PHILOSOPHER ALLAN BLOOM
60

"Values are like fingerprints. Nobody's are the same, but you leave them all over everything you do."
MUSICIAN ELVIS PRESLEY
62

"When your values are clear to you, making decisions becomes easier."
BUSINESS EXECUTIVE ROY E. DISNEY
66

"The decisions you make are a choice of values that reflect your life in every way."
RESTAURATEUR & ACTIVIST ALICE WATERS
70

". . . the core values that underpin sustainable development—interdependence, empathy, equity, personal responsibility and intergenerational justice—are the only foundation upon which any viable vision of a better world can possibly be constructed."
ENVIRONMENTALIST & WRITER JONATHON PORRITT
72

"I think the reward for conformity is that everyone likes you except yourself."
AUTHOR & ACTIVIST RITA MAE BROWN
74

"Culture eats strategy for breakfast."
MANAGEMENT CONSULTANT PETER F. DRUCKER
80

"As you live your values, your sense of identity, integrity, control, and inner-directedness will infuse you with both exhilaration and peace."
AUTHOR STEPHEN COVEY
84

"The CEO is not in charge of the company. The values are. If, at the end of our careers, we have not passed along positive values, we have abdicated our leadership role."
MANAGEMENT CONSULTANT DAVE LOGAN
88

"My goal wasn't to make a ton of money. It was to build good computers."
COMPUTER ENTREPRENEUR STEVE WOZNIAK
90

"Your personal core values define who you are, and a company's core values ultimately define the company's character and brand. For individuals, character is destiny. For organizations, culture is destiny."
INTERNET ENTREPRENEUR TONY HSIEH
92

"An empowered organization is one in which individuals have the knowledge, skill, desire, and opportunity to personally succeed in a way that leads to collective organizational success."
MANAGEMENT CONSULTANT DAVE LOGAN
94

"Values aren't buses. . . . They're not supposed to get you anywhere. They're supposed to define who you are."
AUTHOR JENNIFER CRUSIE
96

"Enlightened leadership is spiritual if we understand spirituality not as some kind of religious dogma or ideology, but as the domain of awareness where we experience values like truth, goodness, beauty, love, and compassion, and also intuition, creativity, insight, and focused attention."
SPIRITUAL LEADER DEEPAK CHOPRA
98

QUOTES
Chapter Four

"A dream is your creative vision for your life in the future. You must break out of your current comfort zone and become comfortable with the unfamiliar and the unknown."
MOTIVATIONAL SPEAKER DENIS WAITLEY
100

"Reality is wrong. Dreams are for real."
MUSICIAN & ENTREPRENEUR TUPAC SHAKUR
102

"Big thinking precedes great achievement."
AUTHOR WILFRED PETERSON
104

"Never doubt that a small group of thoughtful, committed citizens can change the world; indeed, it's the only thing that ever has."
CULTURAL ANTHROPOLOGIST MARGARET MEAD
106

"But if each man could have his own house, a large garden to cultivate and healthy surroundings—then, I thought, there will be for them a better opportunity of a happy family life."
INDUSTRIALIST & PHILANTHROPIST GEORGE CADBURY
108

"You have everything you need to build something far bigger than yourself."
LEADERSHIP EXPERT & ENTREPRENEUR SETH GODIN
112

"Glance at the sun. See the moon and the stars. Gaze at the beauty of Earth's greenings. Now, think."
12TH CENTURY PHILOSOPHER HILDEGARD VON BINGEN
114

"The future of any corporation is as good as the value system of the leaders and followers in the organization."
I.T. INDUSTRIALIST N. R. NARAYANA MURTHY
116

"You cannot change how someone thinks,
but you can give them a tool to use which will
lead them to think differently."

**ARCHITECT & SYSTEMS THEORIST
R. BUCKMINSTER FULLER**

118

"We achieved our mission to the moon. Let's look
home from that lofty perch and reimagine our mission on
Earth—that is what we need to do here. Together, we
can upcycle everything. The world will be better
for our positive visions and actions."

DESIGNER WILLIAM McDONOUGH

122

"Today will never happen again. Don't waste it with a false
start or no start at all. You were not born to fail."

BUSINESS EXPERT & AUTHOR AUGUSTINE "OG" MANDINO

124

"There is something patently insane about all the
typewriters sleeping with all the beautiful plumbing
in the beautiful office buildings, and all the
people sleeping in the slums."

**ARCHITECT & SYSTEMS THEORIST
R. BUCKMINSTER FULLER**

128

"We cannot solve our problems with the same
thinking we used when we created them."

PHYSICIST ALBERT EINSTEIN

130

RESOURCES
Chapter One

BOOKS

The World Is Blue: How Our Fate and the Oceans Are One
Sylvia Earle
National Geographic, 2009

The Fourth Wave: Business in the 21st Century
Herman Maynard and Susan Mehrtens
Berrett-Koehler, 1996

The Blue Sweater: Bridging the Gap between Rich and Poor in an Interconnected World
Jacqueline Novogratz
Rodale Books, 2010

*A More Beautiful Question:
The Power of Inquiry to Spark Breakthrough Ideas*
Warren Berger
Bloomsbury USA, 2014

WEBSITES

Sylvia Earle Alliance
www.mission-blue.org

Pi Day, Exploratorium
www.exploratorium.edu/pi

VIDEOS & ARTICLES

MIT Video 2013 Commencement Address
Drew Houston, Founder of DropBox
MIT TechTV
http://video.mit.edu/watch/mit-commencement-2013-speeches-24832/

"The Science of Character"
Tiffany Schlain, Founder of The Moxie Institute
http://www.youtube.com/watch?v=U3nT2KDAGOc

"Find Your Passion with these 8 Thought-Provoking Questions"
Warren Berger
http://www.fastcodesign.com/3028946/find-your-passion-with-these-8-thought-provoking-questions

RESOURCES
Chapter Two

BOOKS

Nonviolent Communication: A Language of Life (Third Edition)
Marshall B. Rosenberg
Puddledancer Press, 2015

Just Babies: The Origin of Good and Evil
Paul Bloom
Crown, 2013

The Handbook of Organizational Justice (Reprint Edition)
Jerald Greenberg and Jason A. Colquitt, editors
Psychology Press, 2014

Emotional Intelligence 2.0 (Hardcover Edition)
Travis Bradberry and Jeanne Greaves
Talent Smart, 2009

Psychology: A Concise Introduction (Third Edition)
Richard A. Griggs
Worth Publishers, 2010

Human Autonomy in Cross-Cultural Context: Perspectives on the Psychology of Agency, Freedom, and Well-Being
Valery I. Chirkov, Richard M. Ryan, and Kennon M. Sheldon, editors
Springer, 2010

WEBSITES

Drucker Institute
www.druckerinstitute.com

The Center for Nonviolent Communication
www.cnvc.org

Self-Determination Theory:
"An Approach to Human Motivation and Personality"
www.selfdeterminationtheory.org

Online Quiz
Institute for Health and Human Potential:
"Test Your Emotional Intelligence"
http://www.ihhp.com/free-eq-quiz/

Preston Ni Communication Coaching
www.nipreston.com

Preston Ni Communication Success:
"How to Increase Your Emotional Intelligence, 6 Essentials"
https://www.psychologytoday.com/blog/communication-success/ 201410/how-increase-your-emotional-intelligence-6-essentials

Online Quiz
VIA Institute on Character: "Find Your Pathway to Positive"
www.viacharacter.org

MindTools: "What Are Your Values?
Deciding What's Most Important in Life"
https://www.mindtools.com/pages/article/newTED_85.htm

VIDEOS & ARTICLES

Marshall Rosenberg: "Nonviolent Communication:
A Brief Introduction" (Horse Mountain Institute)
https://www.youtube.com/watch?v=DgaeHeIL39Y

Ed Deci: "Promoting Motivation, Health, and Excellence"
(TEDxFlourCity)
https://www.youtube.com/watch?v=VGrcets0E6I

Kris Girrell: "How We've Been Misled by
'Emotional Intelligence'"
(TEDxNatick)
https://www.youtube.com/watch?v=6l8yPt8S2gE

Keene Trial Consulting: "The Workplace Ostracism Scale:
Making the Subjective Objective?"
http://bit.ly/2dyic46

RESOURCES
Chapter Three

BOOKS

Hierarchy of Needs: A Theory of Human Motivation
Abraham Maslow
originally published 1943; available in multiple formats, in print and online

Socrates and Self-Knowledge
Christopher Moore
Cambridge University Press, 2015

The Enneagram Made Easy: Discover the 9 Types of People
Renee Baron and Elizabeth Wagele
HarperOne, 2009

*The Wisdom of the Enneagram:
The Complete Guide to Psychological and Spiritual Growth for the Nine Personality Types (11th Edition)*
Don Richard Riso and Russ Hudson
Bantam, 1999

Just Lucky I Guess: From Closet Lesbian to Radical Dyke
Elaine Mikels
Desert Crone Press, 1994

*Something Incredibly Wonderful Happens:
Frank Oppenheimer and His Astonishing Exploratorium*
K. C. Cole
University of Chicago Press, 2012

WEBSITES

"Conard House: Empowering people who live and work on the margins of society since 1960"
www.conard.org

Online Quiz
VIA Institute on Character: "Find Your Pathway to Positive"
www.viacharacter.org

Sage Journals Abstract:
Social, Psychological & Personality Science:
"On the Contextual Independence of Personality"
Christopher S. Nave, Ryne A. Sherman, David C. Funder,
Sarah E. Hampson, and Lewis R. Goldberg (2010)
http://spp.sagepub.com/content/1/4/327.abstract

The Myers & Briggs Foundation
www.myersbriggs.org

DISCprofile
www.discprofile.com

Online Quiz
"The Big Five Project Personality Test"
www.outofservice.com/bigfive

The Enneagram Institute
www.enneagraminstitute.com

Burning Man
www.burningman.org

VIDEOS & ARTICLES

Jonathan Haidt:
"The moral roots of liberals and conservatives" TED, 2008
https://www.ted.com/talks/jonathan_haidt_on_the_moral_mind?language=en

Daniel Hill, Enneagram Mentor:
"Enneagram Mentoring Video Testimonials & Information"
http://bit.ly/1OlekzC

Excerpt from *Palace of Delights*
(Exploratorium documentary), NOVA, 1982
http://bit.ly/2b3E8Bc

Center for Applications of Psychological Type:
"Personality Type and Stress:
A Coaching Tool for Effective Executive Functioning"
Charles R. Martin, PhD
https://www.capt.org/products/examples/20060HO.pdf

RESOURCES
Chapter Four

BOOKS
*Blue Ocean Strategy, Expanded Edition:
How to Create Uncontested Market Space and Make
the Competition Irrelevant*
W. Chan Kim and Renée Mauborgne
Harvard Business Review Press, 2015

WEBSITES
Encyclopaedia Britannica:
"Henri Breuil, French Archaeologist"
https://www.britannica.com/biography/Henri-Breuil

Lucinda Cross: Founder of the Activate Movement
www.LucindaCross.com

Blue Ocean Strategy
www.blueoceanstrategy.com

VIDEOS & ARTICLES
Community Partnership for Arts and Culture/Reference Desk:
"Strategic Planning Guide"
*http://www.cultureforward.org/Reference-Desk/
Tools/Strategic-Planning*

Harvard Business Review: "Develop Strategic
Thinkers Throughout Your Organization"
Robert Kabacoff, 2014
*https://hbr.org/2014/02/develop-strategic-thinkers-
throughout-your-organization*

AccounTex Report/Tech Trends:
"Business Metrics—Static to Dynamic"
Chuck Vigeant, 2011
https://www.sleeter.com/blog/2011/06/business-metrics/

Inc.: "6 Habits of True Strategic Thinkers"
Paul Schoemaker
*http://www.inc.com/paul-schoemaker/6-habits-
of-strategic-thinkers.html*

Bplans:
"What Is a SWOT Analysis?" Tim Berry
http://articles.bplans.com/how-to-perform-swot-analysis/

businessballs.com: "SWOT Analysis:
SWOT analysis method and examples, with free SWOT template"
http://www.businessballs.com/swotanalysisfreetemplate.htm

PESTLE Analysis:
"Understanding PEST Analysis with Definitions and Examples"
http://pestleanalysis.com/pest-analysis/

MindTools:
"PEST Analysis: Identifying 'Big Picture' Opportunities and Threats"
https://www.mindtools.com/pages/article/newTMC_09.htm

MindTools:
"Gap Analysis: Identifying What Needs to Be Done in a Project"
https://www.mindtools.com/pages/article/gap-analysis.htm

B2C: "3 Examples of Blue Ocean Strategy"
http://bit.ly/2bumYJt

MindTools: "Porter's Five Forces: Assessing the
Balance of Power in a Business Situation"
https://www.mindtools.com/pages/article/newTMC_08.htm

Brian Tracy International: "Strategic Planning Process:
How to Set Long-term Goals"
http://bit.ly/2buo87K

mirum.net: "What Goes in a Competitor Profile?"
http://bit.ly/2bPcoQm

Peter Senge: "Systems Thinking for a Better World"
Aalto Systems Forum, 2014
https://youtu.be/0QtQqZ6Q5-o

William McDonough: "Cradle to Cradle Design"
TED Talks, 2007
https://youtu.be/IoRjz8iTVoo

William McDonough: "Resource Abundance by Design"
World Economic Forum, Tianjin, China, 2014
https://youtu.be/OcO1O99UoUs

www.ingramcontent.com/pod-product-compliance
Lightning Source LLC
Chambersburg PA
CBHW040328300426
44113CB00020B/2693